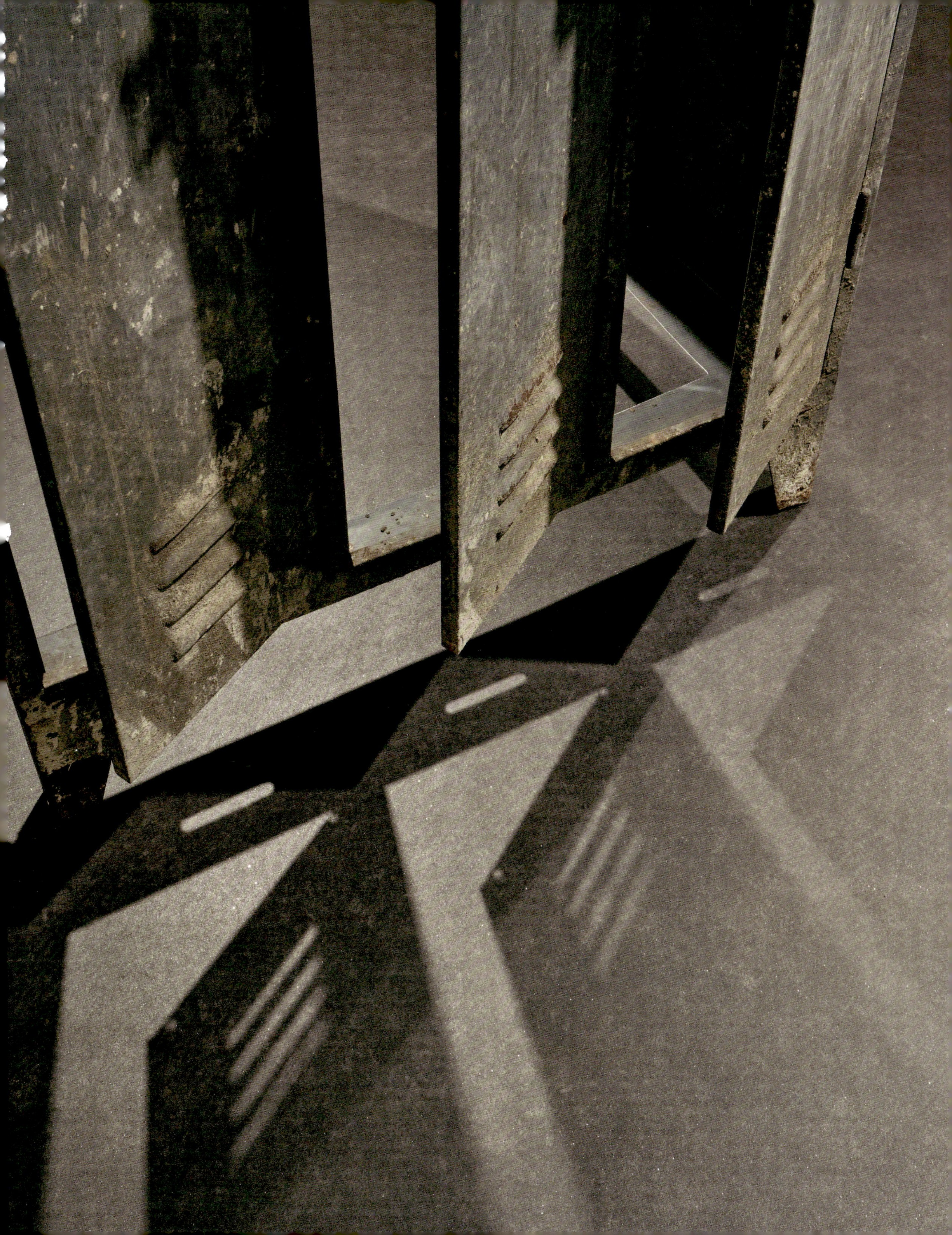

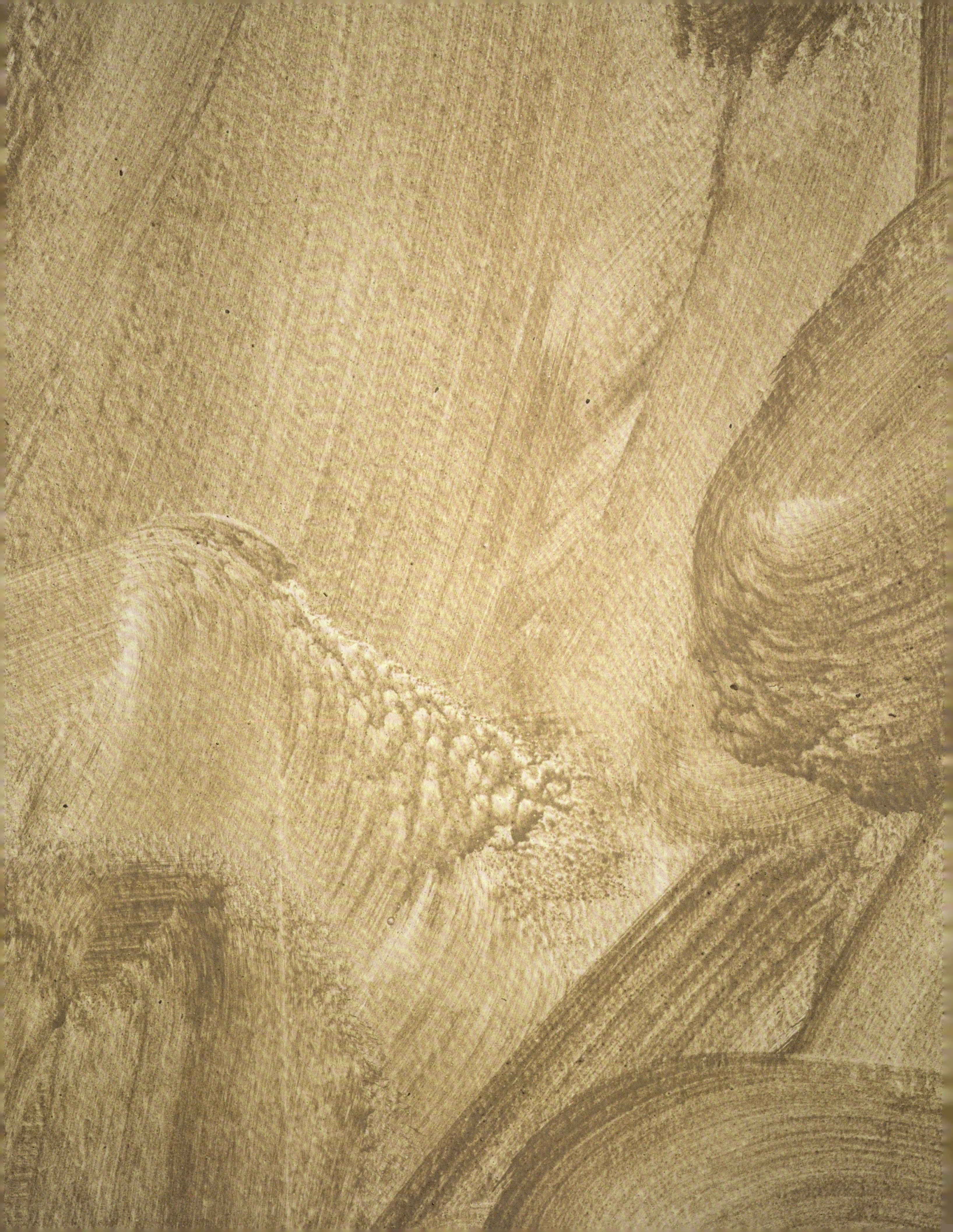

Cache

Luiza Margan

ZF kunststiftung

KERBER ART

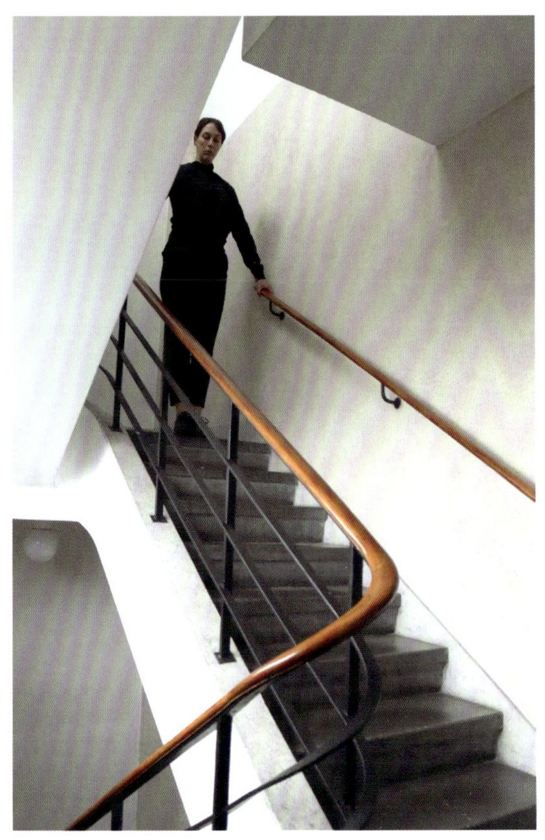

4

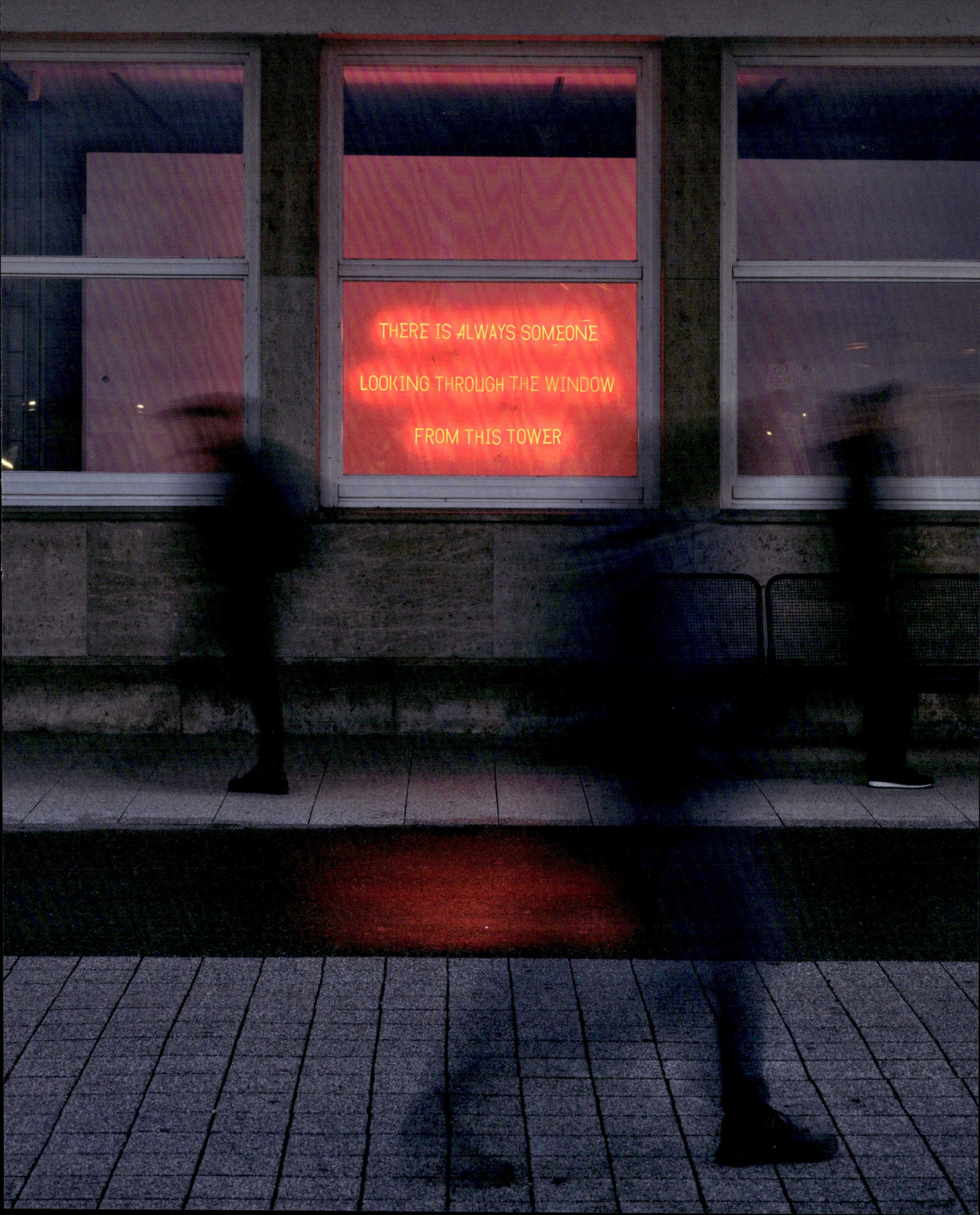
THERE IS ALWAYS SOMEONE
LOOKING THROUGH THE WINDOW
FROM THIS TOWER

Versteckte Zwischenspeicher. Luiza Margans unheimliche Landschaften in uns

6

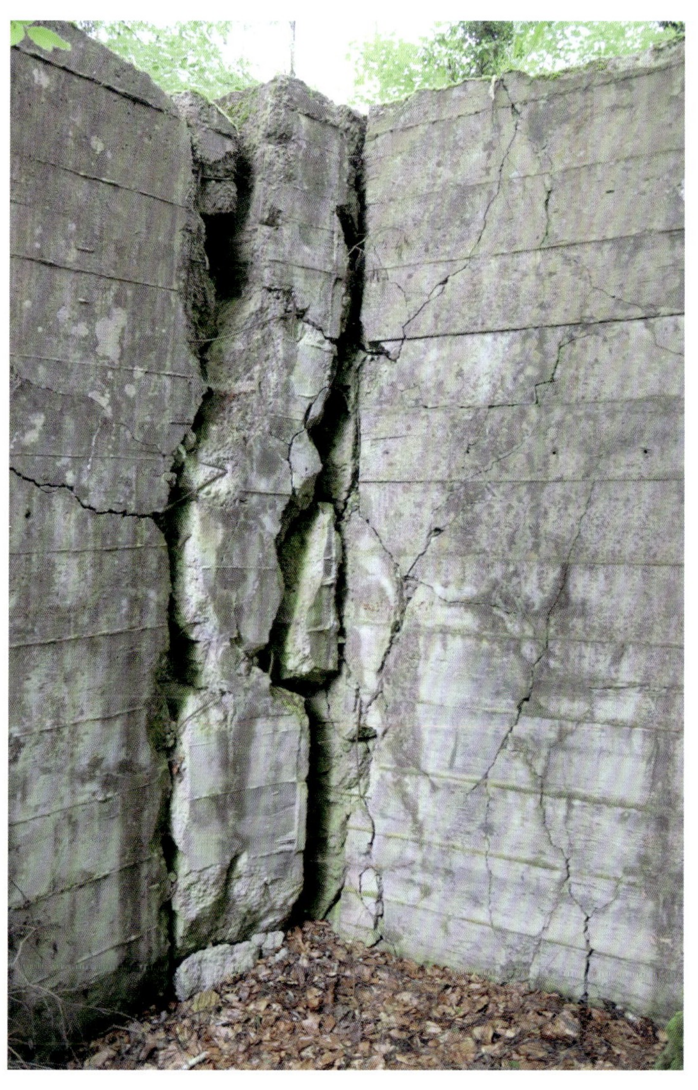

Nora Sternfeld

Nora Sternfeld

Hidden Memory. Luiza Margan's Spectral Landscapes Within Us

Über der wunderschönen Seelandschaft Friedrichshafens thront der Turm des Zeppelin Museums, eines modernistischen Gebäudes, das von 1929 bis 1933 als Hafenbahnhof erbaut wurde – bei seiner Beschreibung wird oft von Bauhaus-Stil oder International Style gesprochen. Heute ist hier ein Museum, das, wie es in der Selbstbeschreibung heißt, „sich den innovativen Prozessen in Technik, Kunst und Gesellschaft verschrieben hat"[1] und als historisches Museum unter anderem die Geschichte des Zeppelins erzählt, während es als zeitgenössischer Kunstraum wechselnde Ausstellungen präsentiert. Ganz oben in diesem Gebäude, mit Ausblick in alle Richtungen, befindet sich ein residency space der ZF Kunststiftung, in dem zeitgenössische Künstler:innen ein Jahr Zeit haben, um etwas zu entwickeln. In diesem Turmatelier hat Luiza Margan viele Monate des letzten Jahres verbracht.

So weit einer der Kontexte, in dem Luiza Margans Ausstellung *Cache* steht, die als Künstlerin selbst immer vom Kontext ausgeht, um ihre künstlerischen Auseinandersetzungen und Untersuchungen zu entwickeln. Ich würde sogar sagen, dass Luiza Margan den Kontext zu ihrem Medium macht, um sich den unheimlichen und verborgenen Geschichten der Orte zu stellen, an denen ihre Arbeiten entstehen, aber auch und vor allem den unheimlichen und verborgenen Geschichten in uns.

Aber was heißt hier Kontext? Ein viel gebrauchtes Wort der Kunst seit den 1960er bzw. spätestens seit den 1990er Jahren[2] wird bei Luiza Margans forschungsbasierten Arbeiten zur körperlichen und materiellen Auseinandersetzung mit dem Unarchivierbaren[3], also mit dem Zwischenraum zwischen der offiziellen Geschichtsschreibung, der marketinggerechten Topografie einerseits und den verborgenen Geschichten und unsichtbaren Machtverhältnissen andererseits. Und genau dieser Zwischenraum ist das Medium der Arbeiten von Luiza Margan, deren genaue Archivarbeit, Feldforschungen und Untersuchungen nichts festmachen, sondern die vielmehr nicht aufhören, nach dem Verschwiegenen, nach dem, was unter der Oberfläche insistiert, zu suchen, und uns einladen, den unheimlichen Dimensionen der Geschichte zu begegnen – eben den unarchivierbaren Kontexten, die die Gegenwart, unsere Sprache und unsere Körper heimsuchen.

1 https://www.zeppelin-museum.de/de/museum/konzept (letzter Zugriff: 15.12.2023)

2 Vgl. Peter Weibel (Hg.), *Kontext Kunst*, Graz 1993.

3 Die Auseinandersetzung mit dem „Unarchivierbaren" war Teil der Forschung des Langzeitprojekts „Spectral Infrastructure" von freethought am BAK in Utrecht, https://www.bakonline.org/program-item/lancering-an-anecdoted-archive-of-exhibition-lives/ (letzter Zugriff: 15.12.2023). Irit Rogoff und ich beschäftigten uns mit dem Unarchivierbaren als das Gespenstische, das das Archiv heimsucht, mit den Mitteln, die einen solchen Spuk ermöglichen, und damit wie eine Arbeit am Unarchivierbaren nicht nur den Inhalt des Archivs, sondern auch das Konzept des Archivs selbst verändern könnte.

Rising high above the beautiful lake landscape around Friedrichshafen is the tower of the Zeppelin Museum, built as a harbor station between 1929 and 1933: modernist architecture often described as the Bauhaus style or International Style. Today it houses a museum dedicated, according to its website, "to innovative processes in technology, art and society,"[1] but also a history museum that tells, not least, the story of the Zeppelin airships, and an exhibition venue for contemporary art. Right at the top of this building, with views in all directions, the ZF Art Foundation runs a residency space where contemporary artists can devote a year to developing a project. Luiza Margan spent many months of the last year in this tower studio.

So much for one of the contexts framing *Cache,* an exhibition by the artist Luiza Margan, who is herself always alive to the context in which her artistic explorations and examinations unfold. I would go so far as to say that Margan has made context her medium, for she confronts not only the hidden and spectral histories of the places where her works evolve but also, and above all, the hidden and spectral histories within us.

But what do we mean here by context? A well-worn notion in art since the 1960s, or at the latest since the 1990s,[2] in Margan's research-based work it underlies a physical and material exploration of the unarchivable,[3] that space that lies between official historiography and marketable topography on the one hand and hidden histories and invisible power relations on the other. It is this space between that supplies the medium for the art of Margan who, with her meticulous digging in archives, her fieldwork and analysis, rather than nailing something down, never stops rooting out the things that are never talked about, the things that mutter insistently below the surface, inviting us to confront the spectral layers of history—those unarchivable contexts that haunt the present, our language, and our bodies.

The first context for her work, then, the place where the process unfolded, is a studio with a view, a place for the production of art. And if we are already talking about sedimented histories, then we can add the history of all the art projects that have emerged here since 1996, and even the history of the work that will emerge here later.

1 https://www.zeppelin-museum.de/en/museum/concept (last accessed December 15, 2023).

2 See Peter Weibel (ed.), *Kontext Kunst*, Graz 1993.

3 An analysis of "the unarchivable" formed part of the research for the long-term project "Spectral Infrastructure" by freethought at the BAK in Utrecht, https://www.bakonline.org/program-item/lancering-an-anecdoted-archive-of-exhibition-lives (last accessed December 15, 2023). Irit Rogoff and I explored the unarchivable as a spectral force that haunts the archive, the procedures that make the haunting possible, and hence how working with the unarchivable might change not only the content of an archive, but the very concept of an archive.

A residency, after all, always draws together two perspectives: the artistic view from outside, and the place on which it falls. In this sense, another context for the work—and this is always an important factor in her situated, embodied practice—is Luiza Margan herself, her view and her history. She allows her artistic production to grow out of the hidden dimensions of her context and brings its echo to the space into which she then invites us. Because we are certainly part of the context too, each of us an observer with a personal biography and history. It is also about what we infer when we read the big red neon letters on the window of the exhibition room:

"THERE IS ALWAYS SOMEONE
LOOKING THROUGH THE WINDOW
FROM THIS TOWER"[4]

In this respect, Luiza Margan's installations are situated questionings.[5] Around the exhibition *Cache* we can follow them in concentric circles. First of all, the investigation that we encounter here is situated in this tower, in a studio belonging to the ZF Art Foundation,[6] whose "commitment to art and culture" is a "fixed element of the company's corporate identity,"[7] in a building which did not simply formulate modernism in spatial terms but integrated traces of an unspoken entanglement with ethnicist identities and perhaps even design elements borrowed from fascist futurism: the modernist transit zone suggests, especially in the stairwell, dynamic lines and jagged forms, while its layout quotes architectures of surveillance. The building as a whole is doubtless imbued by the spirit of its time: 1933, the year the new harbor station opened, was the year when the National Socialists came to power.

More broadly, the questioning is situated in Friedrichshafen, a German town on Lake Constance with an unbounded pride in the history of the Zeppelin: a town which, perhaps like many towns in Germany, or at least those where the arms industry played

4 This sentence is a kind of "residue of the day" from Luiza Margan's reading matter during her residency. It comes from the publication: CONNY, Fion Pellacini, Karimah Ashadu, Nina Kuttler, Nina Zeljkovic, *Reisestipendien 2021,* ed. Eva Birkenstock (Neue Kunst in Hamburg e. V.), Hamburg 2021, https://www.textem-verlag.de/textem/kunst/487 (last accessed December 15, 2023).

5 See Donna Haraway, "Situated Knowledges: The Science Question in Feminism and the Privilege of Partial Perspective", in: *Feminist Studies* 3 (1988), pp. 575–599, http://www.staff.amu.edu.pl/~ewa/Haraway,%20Situated%20Knowledges.pdf (last accessed October 31, 2023).

6 Information page on the Foundation website, https://zf-kunststiftung.com/en/foundation/information/ (last accessed December 15, 2023). "The ZF Art Foundation was established in 1990. To mark ZF Friedrichshafen AG's 75th anniversary, the company began exploring new ways of fulfilling its commitment to art and culture, which is a fixed element of the company's corporate identity. ZF wanted to make a statement and create a permanent institution which would be of benefit for the people of the Lake Constance region that is also home to many of ZF's employees."

Der erste Kontext der Arbeit, da sie ja dort im Prozess entwickelt wurde, ist also ein Atelier mit Ausblick, ein Ort der Kunstproduktion. Und wenn wir nun schon von sedimentierten Geschichten ausgehen, dann können wir sagen, es ist auch die Geschichte aller künstlerischen Projekte, die seit 1996 hier entstanden sind, und sogar die Geschichte der Arbeiten, die nachher hier entstehen werden. Denn bei einer Residency treffen immer zwei Perspektiven zusammen: der künstlerische Blick von außen und der Ort, auf den er fällt. In diesem Sinne stellt einen weiteren Kontext der Arbeit – und das ist für ihre situierte, verkörperte Praxis immer wichtig – Luiza Margan selbst dar, ihr Blick und ihre Geschichte. So lässt sie ihre künstlerische Produktion aus den verborgenen Dimensionen ihres Kontexts erwachsen und bringt sie als Echo in den Raum, in den sie uns wiederum einlädt. Denn Kontext, das sind sicherlich auch wir – der Lebenslauf und die Geschichten der jeweiligen Betrachter:innen. Es geht also auch um das, was wir mitlesen, wenn wir an der Scheibe des Ausstellungsraums in großen roten Neon-Lettern lesen:

„THERE IS ALWAYS SOMEONE
LOOKING THROUGH THE WINDOW
FROM THIS TOWER"[4]

Die Installationen Luiza Margans sind in diesem Sinne situierte Auseinandersetzungen.[5] Folgen wir ihnen im Zusammenhang mit der Ausstellung *Cache* in konzentrischen Kreisen: Situiert ist die Untersuchung, der wir hier begegnen, zuerst in diesem Turm, in einem Atelier der ZF Kunststiftung[6], deren „Engagement für Kunst und Kultur" fester „Bestandteil der Corporate Identity" ist[7], in einem Gebäude, das nicht nur die Moderne in den Raum stellte, sondern auch Spuren von deren verdrängter Verstrickung mit völkischen Selbstverständnissen oder gar von Gestaltungselementen des faschistischen Futurismus trägt – der modernistische Transitraum suggeriert

4 Der Satz ist so etwas wie ein „Tagesrest" einer Lektüre Luiza Margans während ihrer Residency. Er stammt aus der Publikation: CONNY, Fion Pellacini, Karimah Ashadu, Nina Kuttler, Nina Zeljkovic, *Reisestipendien 2021,* hrsg. v. Eva Birckenstock (Neue Kunst in Hamburg e. V.), Hamburg 2021, https://www.textem-verlag.de/textem/kunst/487 (letzter Zugriff: 15.12.2023).

5 Vgl. Donna Haraway, „Situated Knowledges: The Science Question in Feminism and the Privilege of Partial Perspective", in: *Feminist Studies,* 3, 1988, S. 575–599, http://www.staff.amu.edu.pl/~ewa/Haraway,%20Situated%20Knowledges.pdf (letzter Zugriff: 31.10.2023)

6 Informationstext der Stiftung, https://zf-kunststiftung.com/stiftung/information/ (letzter Zugriff: 31.10.2023). „Die ZF Kunststiftung wurde 1990 gegründet. Die ZF Friedrichshafen AG feierte in dem Jahr ihr 75-jähriges Bestehen. Das Jubiläum war ein willkommener Anlass, um das Engagement für Kunst und Kultur, das fester Bestandteil der Corporate Identity ist, in neue Bahnen zu lenken. ZF wollte ein Zeichen setzen und eine Institution ins Leben rufen, die Bestand hat und den Menschen in der Bodenseeregion, zu denen ja auch viele ZF-Mitarbeiter gehören, langfristig zugutekommt."

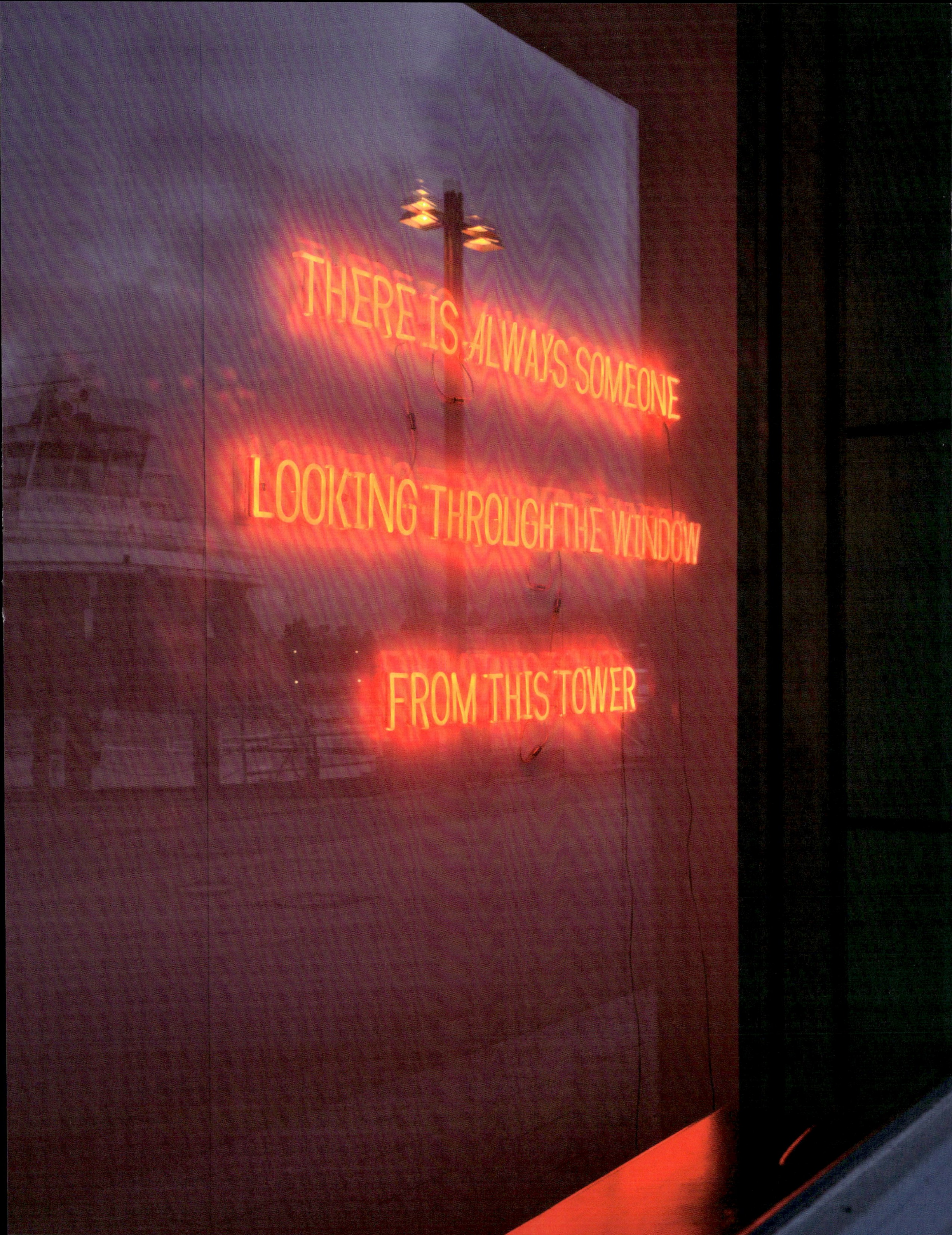
THERE IS ALWAYS SOMEONE
LOOKING THROUGH THE WINDOW
FROM THIS TOWER

vor allem im Stiegenhaus dynamische Linien und gezackte Formen, seine Anlage zitiert Überwachungsarchitekturen. Das Gebäude steht insgesamt sicherlich im Geiste seiner Zeit: Im Eröffnungsjahr des neuen Hafenbahnhofs 1933 kamen die Nationalsozialisten an die Macht.

Situiert ist die Auseinandersetzung des Weiteren in Friedrichshafen: Eine deutsche Stadt am Bodensee, geprägt von ihrem unbändigen Stolz auf die Geschichte des Zeppelins, eine Stadt, die sich wie vielleicht viele Städte in Deutschland, jedenfalls solche, in denen die Waffenindustrie eine Rolle spielte und spielt, dieser Geschichte und Gegenwart zugleich stellt, deren Erinnerung, sich der Auseinandersetzung aber doch auch immer wieder entledigt, vielleicht sogar mit den Mitteln der Kunst. So geht es in der Arbeit von Luiza Margan eben um Kontext als Einladung, uns dem Unheimlichen in Vergangenheit und Gegenwart, dem Unheimlichen in uns zu stellen. Dafür gräbt Luiza Margan dort, wo die Residency sie hinführte: im Boden der unheimlichen Landschaft des Friedrichshafener Ortsteils Raderach. Im Raderacher Forst wurden 1942 ein Prüfwerk mit drei Raketen-Testständen und ein Sauerstoffwerk[8] errichtet. Hier wurden Teile für die sogenannte „Wunderwaffe", die V2-Rakete der Firma Luftschiffbau Zeppelin in Friedrichshafen, getestet. In Oberraderach befand sich auch ein KZ-Außenlager von Dachau – vom 22. Juni 1943 bis 29. September 1944 waren hier über 1200 Menschen inhaftiert, die für den Bau der A4-Halbschalen beim Luftschiffbau Zeppelin eingesetzt wurden.[9] Luiza Margan bringt Erde von dort, wo das Barackenlager stand, in den Ausstellungsraum. Das geht wohl nicht, ohne sich die Hände schmutzig zu machen, und nicht, ohne die Weiße des Ausstellungsraumes zu stören, dessen Wände sie mit der Erde von Raderach so bemalt, dass die schlammige Textur sichtbar bleibt.

Auf der Suche nach der Geschichte auf dem Gelände von Raderach erscheint dieses der Künstlerin wie eine merkwürdig unmarkierte Ruine. Während sie deren Spuren folgt, stellt sie fest, dass es sich um ein „Geheimprojekt" handelte, nicht nur, weil es ein Lager war, sondern auch, weil die Entwicklung der Rakete und die damit verbundenen Tests nicht öffentlich werden sollten. Und doch, so findet sie heraus, waren diese offenbar so laut, dass sie über den gesamten Bodensee bis in die Schweiz hörbar waren – ein

7 Mehr zum Kontext der ZF Friedrichshafen AG: https://www.waffenvombodensee.com/zf-friedrichshafen/, zu deren Selbstbeschreibung siehe auch hier: www.zf.com (letzter Zugriff auf beide Seiten: 15.12.2023)

8 Vgl. http://www.kz-gedenkstaette-friedrichshafen.de/don/KZ.htm (letzter Zugriff: 15.12.2023)

9 Vgl. Christa Tholander, „Als Dachau im Juni 1943 nach Friedrichshafen kam – KZ-Häftlinge, die V2 und das Unternehmen Luftschiffbau Zeppelin GmbH". In: *Friedrichshafener Jahrbuch für Geschichte und Kultur,* 6 (2014), S. 176–235.

and still plays a role, acknowledges its past and present, the memory of them, but which again and again hands over the questioning, possibly even with the aid of art. Luiza Margan's work presents context as an invitation to confront the spectres of the past and present, and the spectres in ourselves. To this end Luiza Margan digs where the residency took her: in the soil of the spectral landscape of Raderach, a district of Friedrichshafen. In 1942 a test site was built in Raderach Forest, with three test stands for missiles and an oxygen factory.[8] Components were tested here for the "Wunderwaffe," the V-2 rocket built in Friedrichshafen by the airship manufacturer Luftschiffbau Zeppelin. In Oberraderach there was also a satellite of the Dachau concentration camp. From June 22, 1943 until September 29, 1944, it had more than 1200 inmates; they provided the labor to build the A4 semi-monocoques for the Luftschiffbau Zeppelin.[9] Luiza Margan brings soil from the place where the camp huts once stood into the exhibition space. It's not possible to do that without getting your hands dirty or tainting the whiteness of the exhibition space. Its walls are daubed with earth from Raderach in such a way that the muddy texture remains visible.

In her search for history on the Raderach site, the artist discovers a strangely unmarked ruin. As she follows the traces, she realizes that this was a "secret project," not only because of the camp, but because the missile development and the associated tests were not to be made public. And yet, she learns, these activities were apparently so loud that they could be heard right across the lake and into Switzerland—a deafening silence, then, which the artist investigates further. At the same time, nobody claims to have known what was going on… She writes: "It is (is it?) hard to (want to) mark something that was a secret back then (not a long time ago). Is it better to leave it as a secret, even now? Who does it concern? To whom does the secret belong? And what does it mean if we do not know that it is there?"[10]

So in her research Luiza Margan addresses the silence and the secret which, once we begin to hear it, refuses to stop insisting on the present. Not only does she hunt down the hidden contexts for the crimes and violence; she also seeks out traces and evidence of resistance. She comes across a little group of courageous

7 More about the context for ZF Friedrichshafen AG can be found in German on the website of the campaign group GEGEN WAFFEN VOM BODENSEE: https://www.waffenvombodensee.com/zf-friedrichshafen/. The company itself describes its operations here: https://www.zf.com/mobile/en/homepage/homepage.html (both sites last accessed December 15, 2023).

8 For more (in German), see http://www.kz-gedenkstaette-friedrichshafen.de/don/KZ.htm (last accessed December 15, 2023).

9 See Christa Tholander, "Als Dachau im Juni 1943 nach Friedrichshafen kam – KZ-Häftlinge, die V2 und das Unternehmen Luftschiffbau Zeppelin GmbH," in: *Friedrichshafener Jahrbuch für Geschichte und Kultur* 6 (2014), pp. 176–235.

activists with roots in the labor movement. By consulting archives, and thanks to the knowledge and work of local historians and history campaigners, Luiza Margan finds out, for example, about the resistance fighters Georg Elser and Fridolin Endrass; the latter was caught by the National Socialists when he was carrying leaflets in his bicycle tires on the way back from Switzerland. She is curious about how information changed hands, about how people communicated with each other, risking their freedom and their lives. Their hiding places and their endeavors, the incessant danger, the secret places and routes, the whispering in the hope of liberation: these were important inspirations for her work on the exhibition. Secrecy becomes spectral installation material. We cannot grasp it directly, but perhaps we will meet it in these lockers set between the brown walls.

The deconstructed lockers function as partitions. They were reconstructed from classic industrial relics, severed and pieced back together—lockers made by workers for workers, opening and closing themselves and the space. Luiza Margan treats them as “bodies,” as containers with an inside and an outside, some prominent and others less so. They conceal and display anti-fascist books, offer clues to the hiding places and the leaflets, because Luiza Margan has carved words in the metal: words such as “eyes open,” “resistance,” and “freedom,” the typography and wording copied straight from original German and international anti-Nazi postcards, leaflets, and resistance texts. Just as the partitions open and close space, displaying and concealing at once, so the walls signal and break open the silencing. Here, four black bicycle tires cut through white insulation foam. Luiza Margan calls these assemblages “silent landscapes” and “defective soundproofing.” The silence of the landscape seems to be shattered by the assemblages, criss-crossed by pathways of resistance.

A cache is a hidden store. It is also the hidden interim memory in our digital devices: the cache contains the information “remembered” by the computer after it has seemingly disappeared. For a while, then, something is both hidden and saved. The situated practice of Luiza Margan exposes a landscape of violent histories which

10 Email from Luiza Margan to Nora Sternfeld, October 28, 2023.

11

ohrenbetäubendes Stillschweigen also, dem die Künstlerin forschend nachgeht. Zugleich wollte niemand gewusst haben, was hier geschah … Sie schreibt: „Es ist schwer, etwas kennzeichnen zu wollen, das damals (vor nicht allzu langer Zeit) ein Geheimnis war. Ist es vielleicht besser, es auch jetzt im Geheimen zu lassen? Wen betrifft es? Wem gehört das Geheimnis? Und was bedeutet es, wenn wir nicht wissen, dass es da ist?“[10]

Bei ihren Recherchen beschäftigt sich Luiza Margan also mit dem Schweigen und dem Geheimnis, das, wenn wir es zu hören beginnen, nicht aufhören kann, in der Gegenwart zu insistieren. Dabei widmet sie sich nicht nur den verborgenen Kontexten der Verbrechen und der Gewalt, sie sucht auch nach Spuren und Überlieferungen des Widerstands. Bei ihren Recherchen begegnet sie einer kleinen Gruppe mutiger Aktivist:innen, die aus der Arbeiter:innenbewegung hervorgingen. Luiza Margan erfährt in Archiven und dank des Wissens und der Arbeit lokaler Historiker:innen und Geschichtsaktivist:innen zum Beispiel von den Widerstandskämpfern Georg Elser und Fridolin Endraß. Letzterer wurde von den Nationalsozialisten gefasst, als er Flugblätter in den Reifen seines Fahrrads transportierte, mit dem er aus der Schweiz zurückfuhr. Sie beschäftigt sich mit dem Informationsaustausch, mit der Art und Weise, wie die Menschen miteinander kommunizierten und dabei ihre Freiheit und ihr Leben riskierten. Ihre Verstecke und Anstrengungen, die ständigen Gefahren, die geheimen Orte und Wege, das Geflüster in der Hoffnung auf Freiheit waren eine wichtige Inspiration für die Arbeiten an der Ausstellung. Das Geheime wird wiederum zum unheimlichen Material der Installation. Wir können es nicht direkt fassen, aber wir können ihm vielleicht in den Spinden begegnen, die inmitten der braunen Wände stehen.

Die dekonstruierten Spinde fungieren als Raumteiler. Sie sind eine durchschnittene und wieder zusammengesetzte Rekonstruktion von klassischen alten Industriearbeiten – Spinde von Arbeiter:innen für Arbeiter:innen, die sich selbst und den Raum öffnen und schließen. Luiza Margan versteht sie als „Körper“, als Behälter mit einem Innen und einem Außen, mal mehr, mal weniger exponiert. Sie bergen und präsentieren antifaschistische Bücher, verweisen auf die Verstecke und auf die Flugblätter, denn

10 In einer E-Mail von Luiza Margan an Nora Sternfeld vom 28.10.2023.

in das Metall hat Luiza Margan etwas eingeschrieben: Worte wie „Augen Auf“, „Widerstand“ oder „Freiheit“, deren Typografie und Wortlaut sie direkt aus historischen deutschen und internationalen antinazistischen Postkarten, Flugblättern und Widerstandsschriften übernommen hat. So wie die Raumteiler, die den Raum öffnen und schließen, zugleich zeigen und verstecken, wird auch an den Wänden die Stillstellung zugleich thematisiert und aufgebrochen. An den Wänden schneiden vier schwarze Fahrradschläuche durch weißen, schalldichten Schaumstoff. Luiza Margan nennt diese Assemblagen „stille Landschaften“ und „ein gestörtes schalldämmendes System“. So scheint das Schweigen der stillen Landschaft also durch die Assemblagen gebrochen, durchkreuzt durch Wege des Widerstands.

Cache ist eine Bezeichnung für den „versteckten Zwischenspeicher“ unserer Geräte, im Cache ist das, was sich der Computer merkt, wenn es eigentlich nicht mehr da ist. Für eine Zeit ist also etwas zugleich versteckt und gespeichert. Die situierte Praxis Luiza Margans legt eine Landschaft von zugleich schweigenden und schreienden Gewaltgeschichten frei, die zeitlich gar nicht so weit zurückliegen und politisch in verschiedenen Strömungen im heutigen Europa weiterwirken. So widmet sie ihre Arbeit diesem unarchivierbaren unheimlich-untoten Wissen, das eher insistiert als existiert. Sie fördert dabei nicht nur Unarchiviertes zutage, um neues Archivmaterial hinzuzufügen – vielmehr bringt sie das Insistieren des Unarchivierbaren zum Vibrieren, macht es unleugbar, ohne es sich zurechtzulegen, ohne es zu simulieren oder zu verwerten.

are both silent and piercingly loud, which do not lie so very far back in the past, and which are still a force within various political movements in Europe today. Thus she dedicates her work to this unarchivable, hauntingly undead knowledge, insistent rather than existent. In so doing she not only unearths unarchived material to add to the archives, but prods away at the insistent muttering of the unarchivable until it breaks into a hum, making it undeniable without ordering it neatly, simulating it, or turning it into a product.

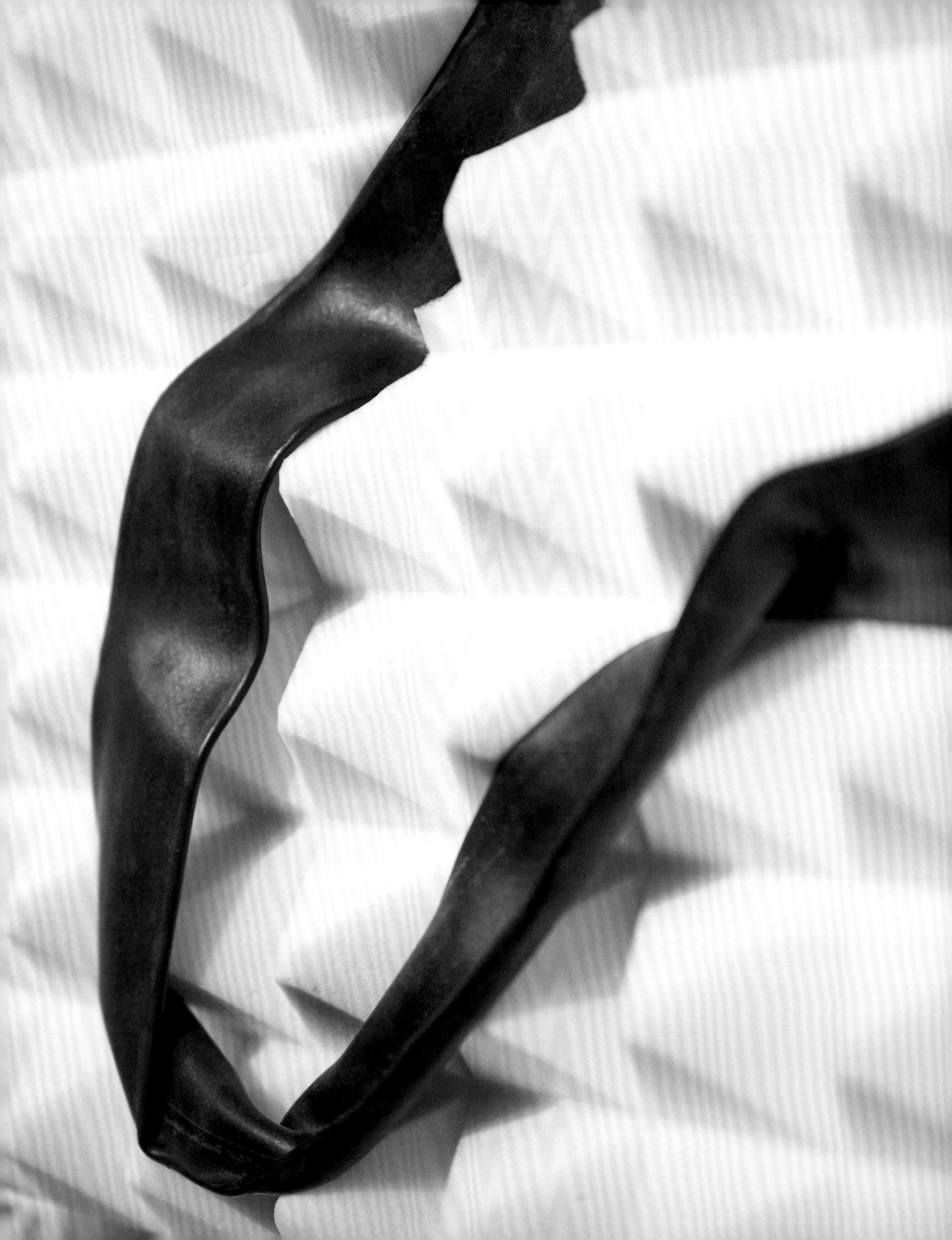

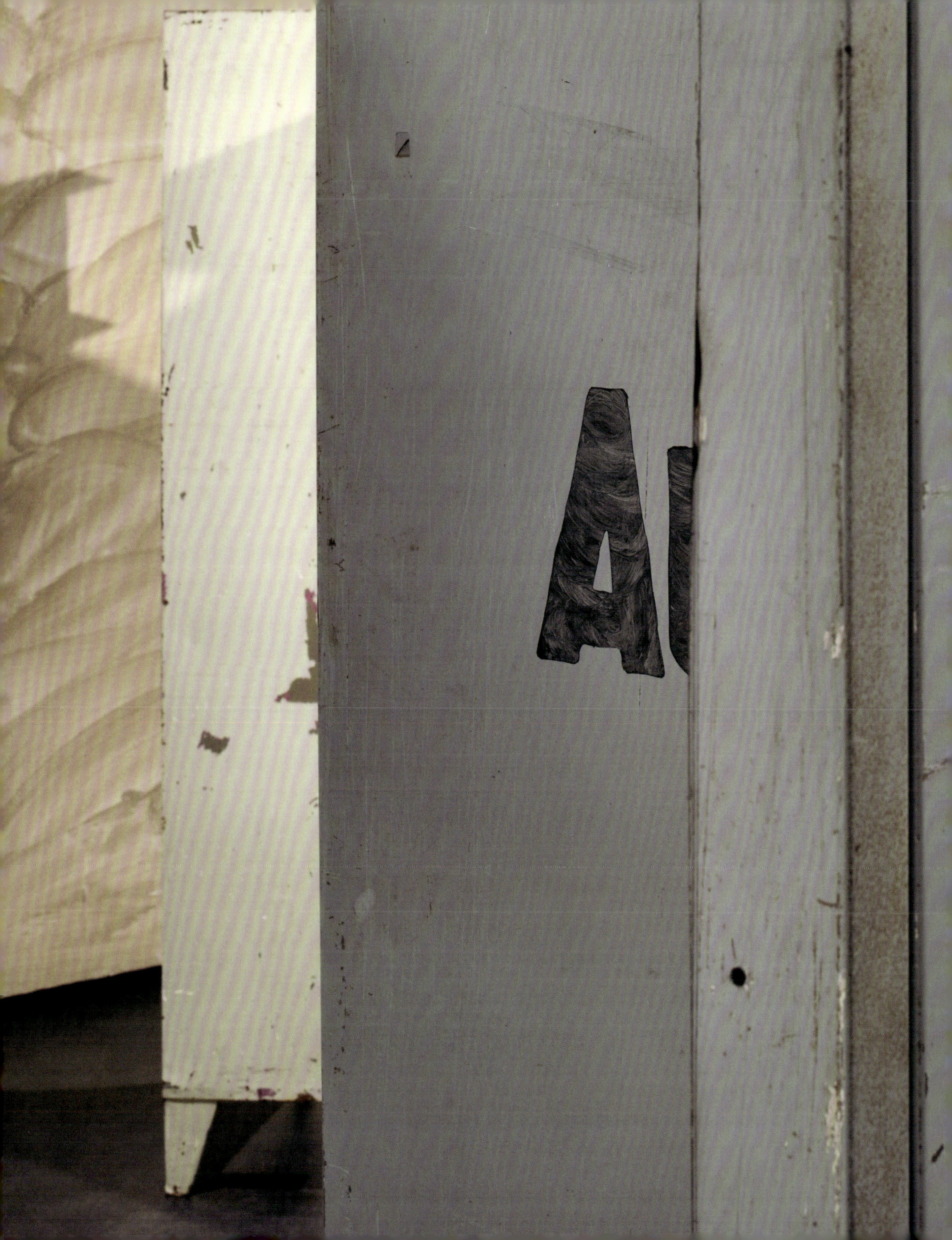

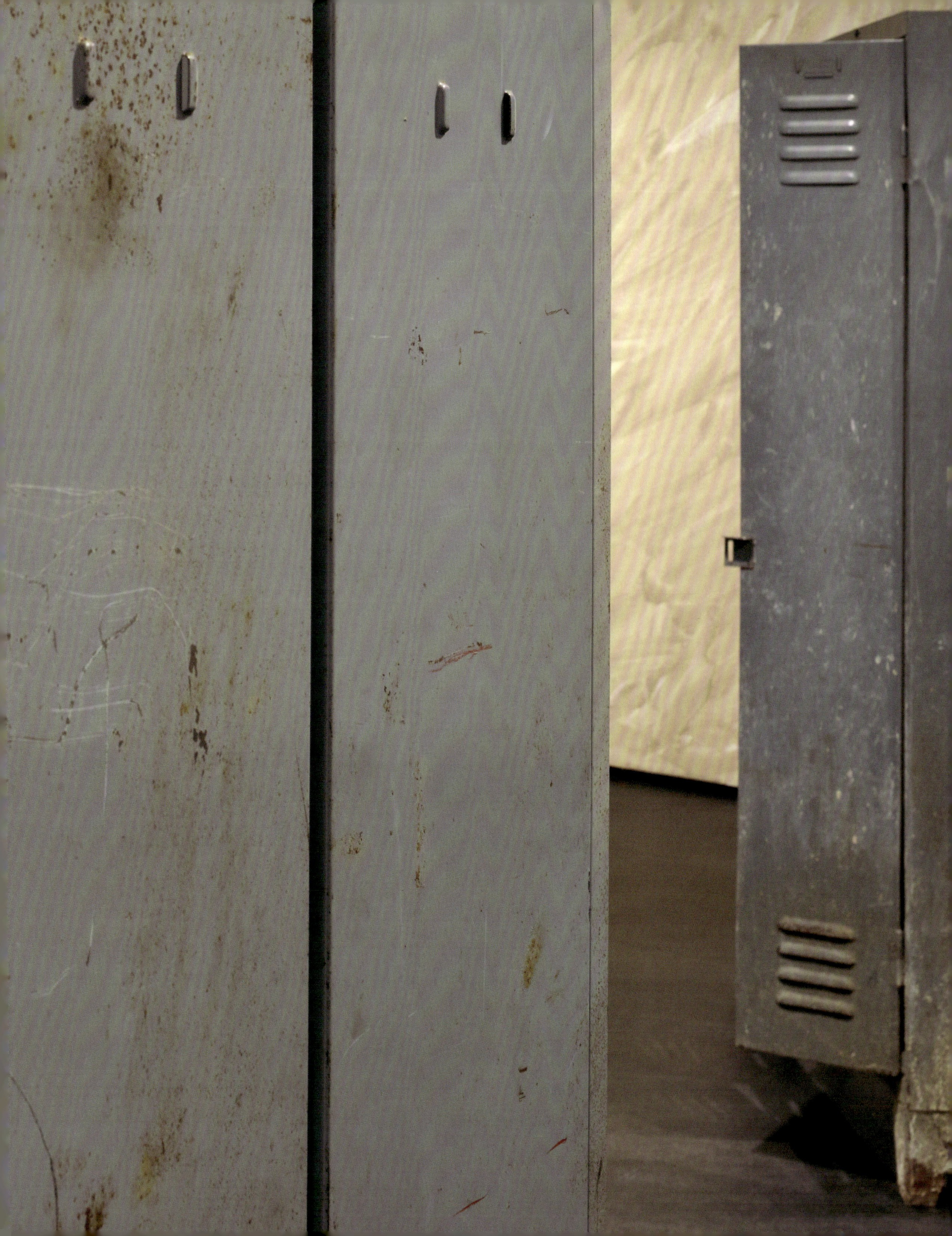

16

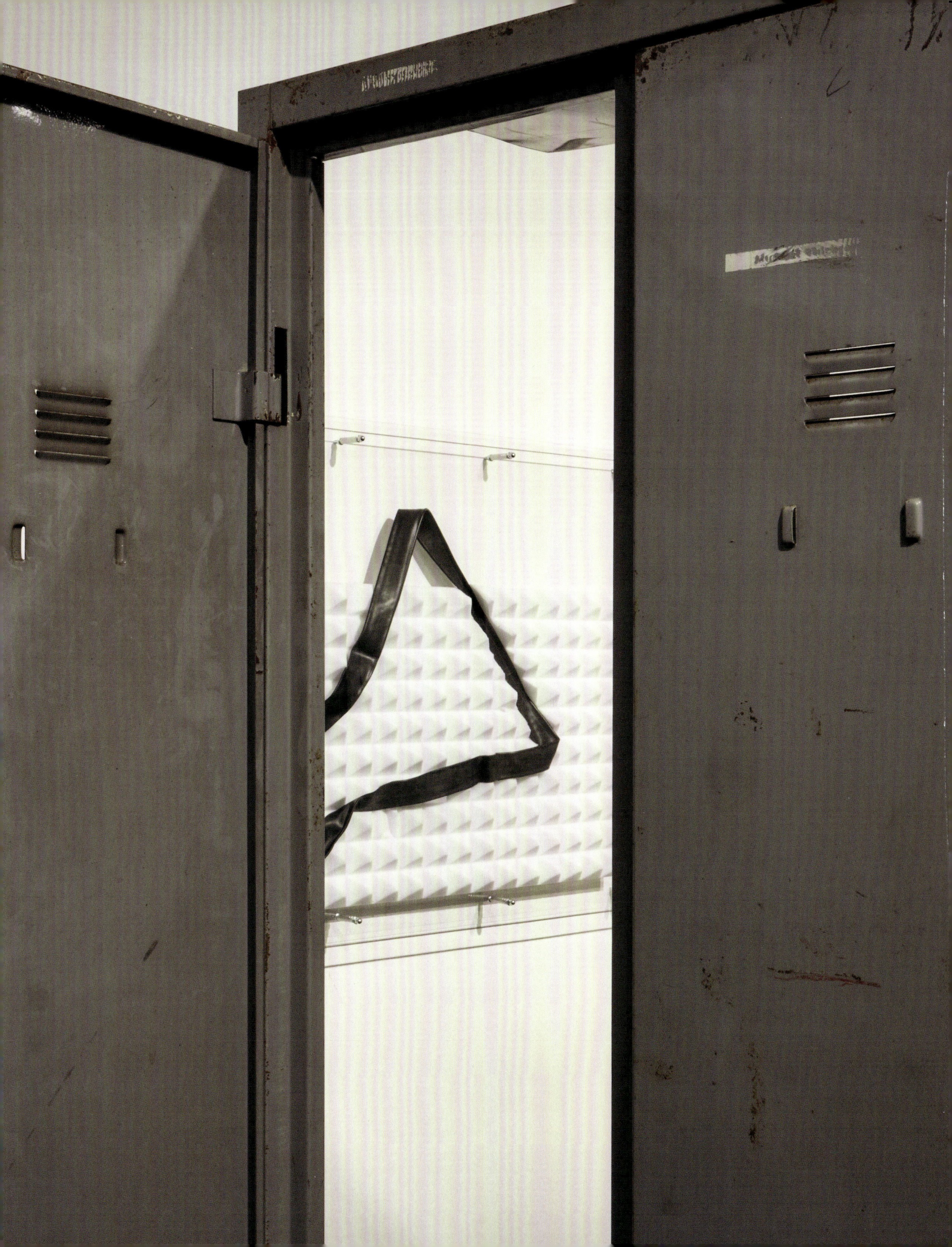

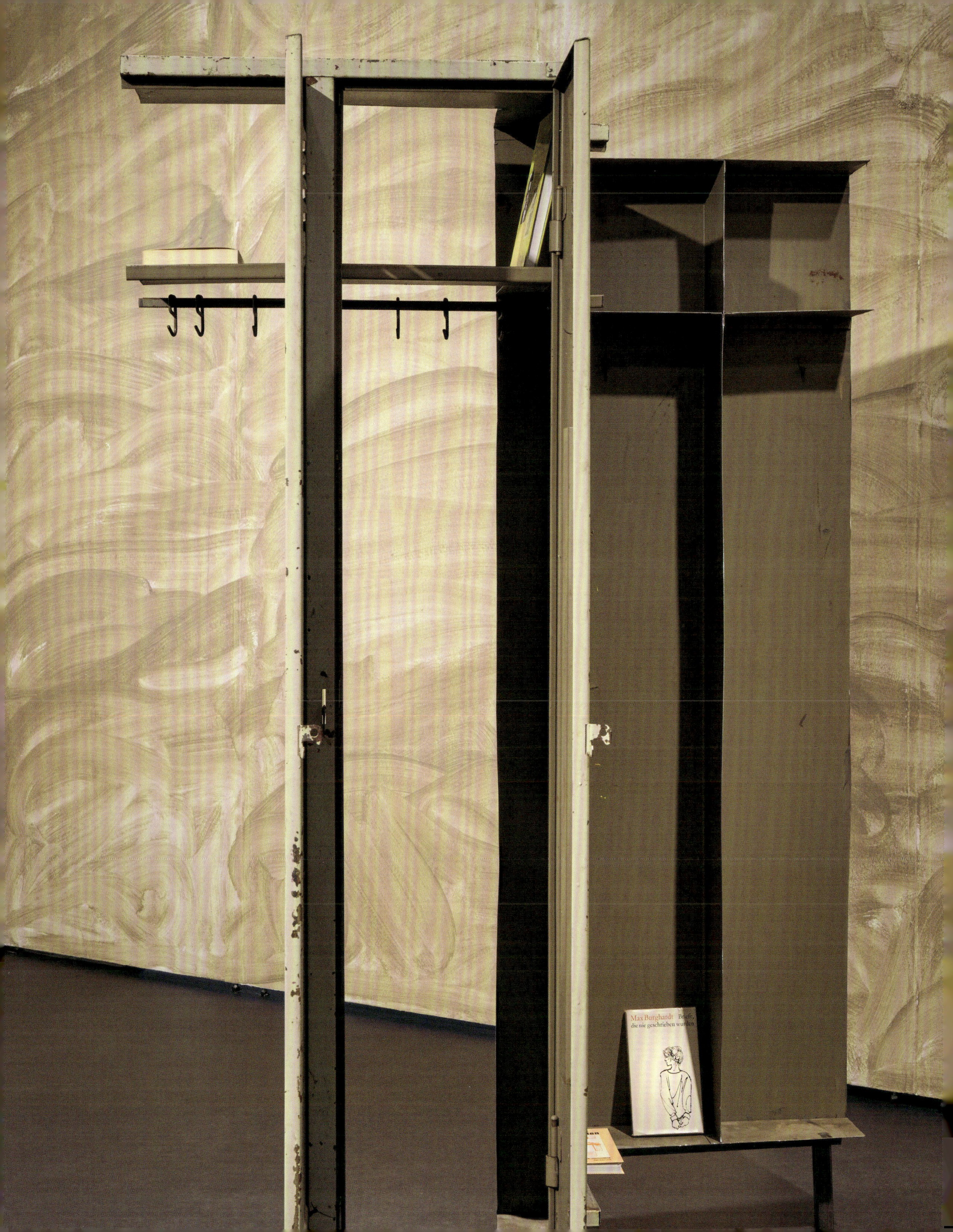
Max Burghardt Briefe,
die nie geschrieben

19

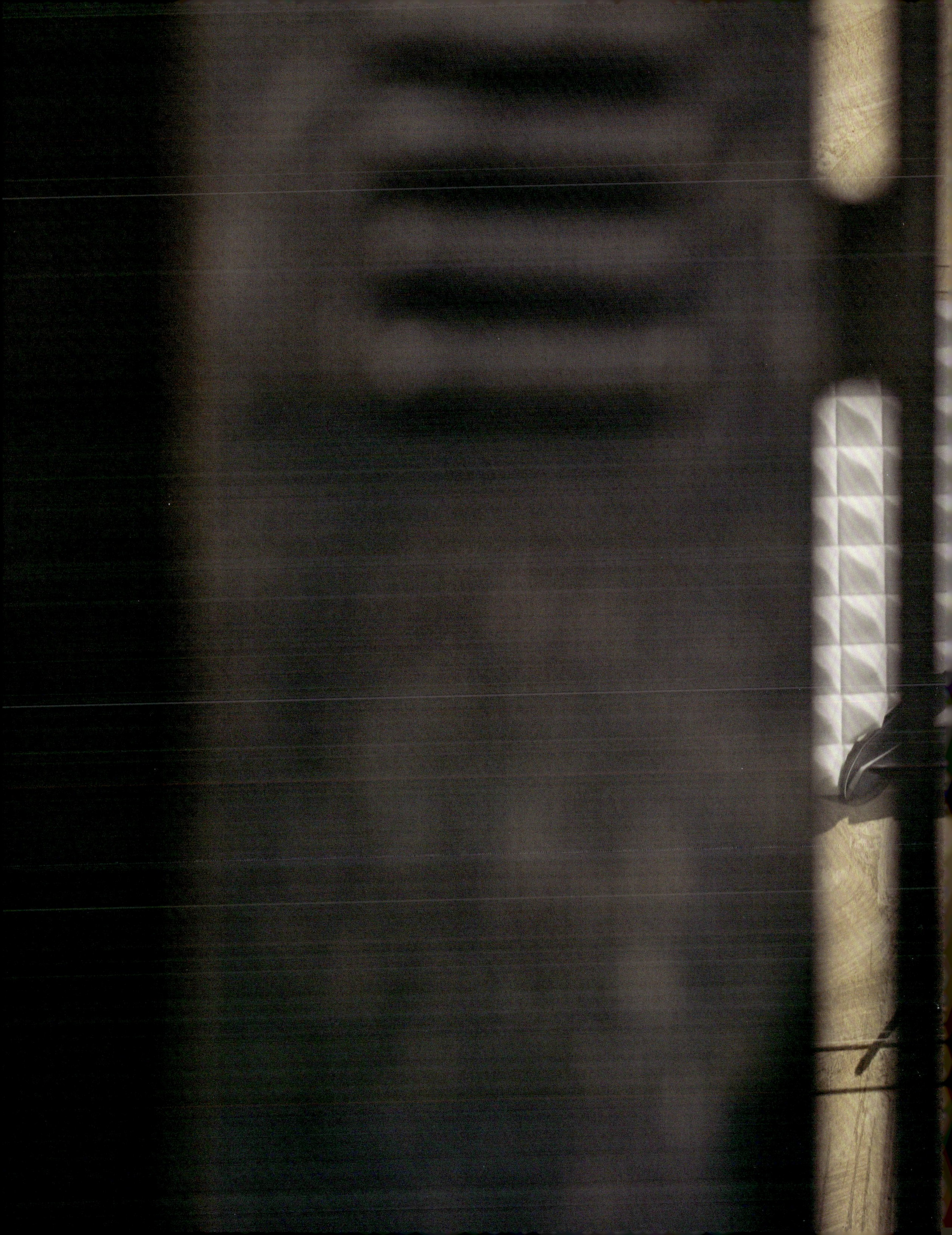

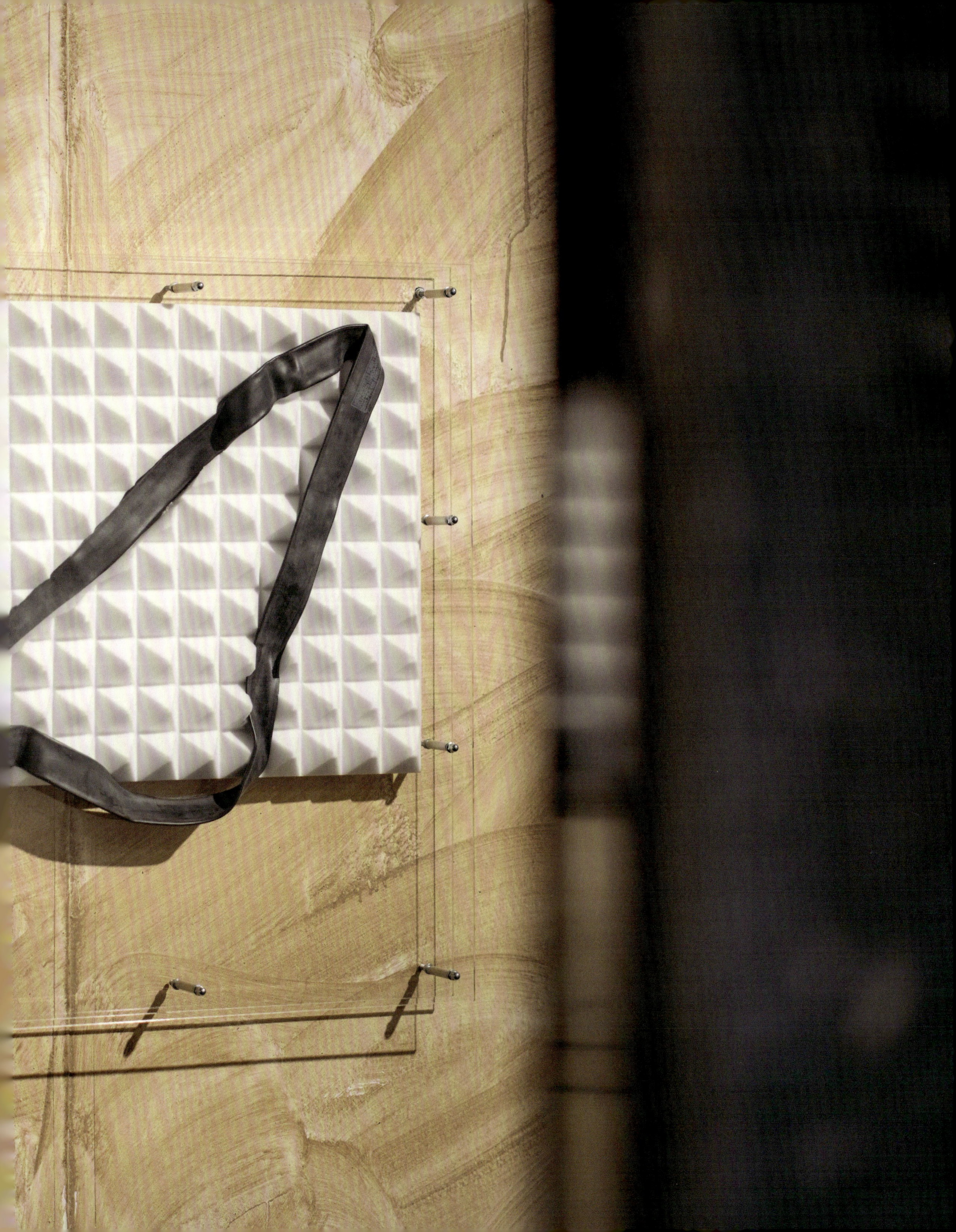

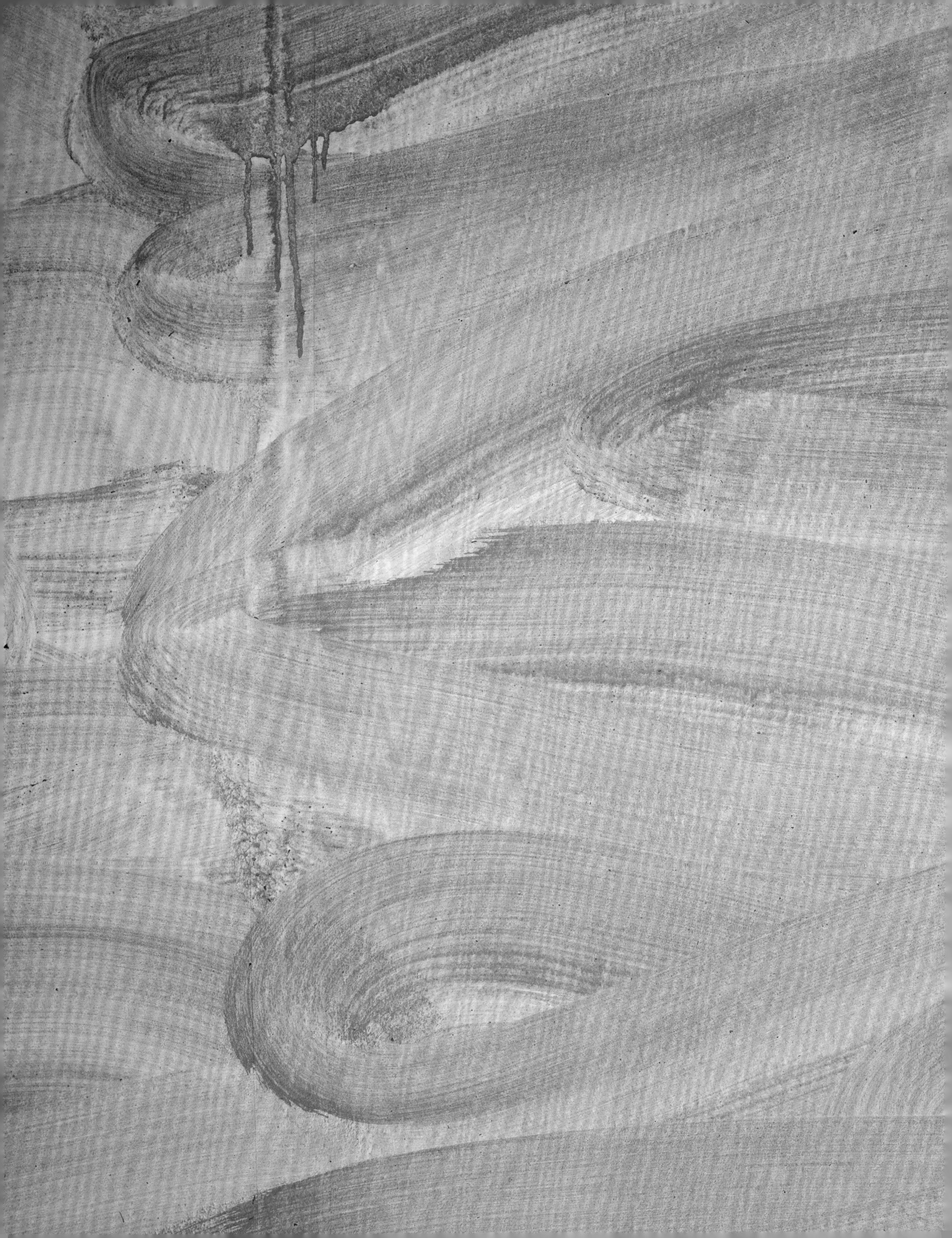

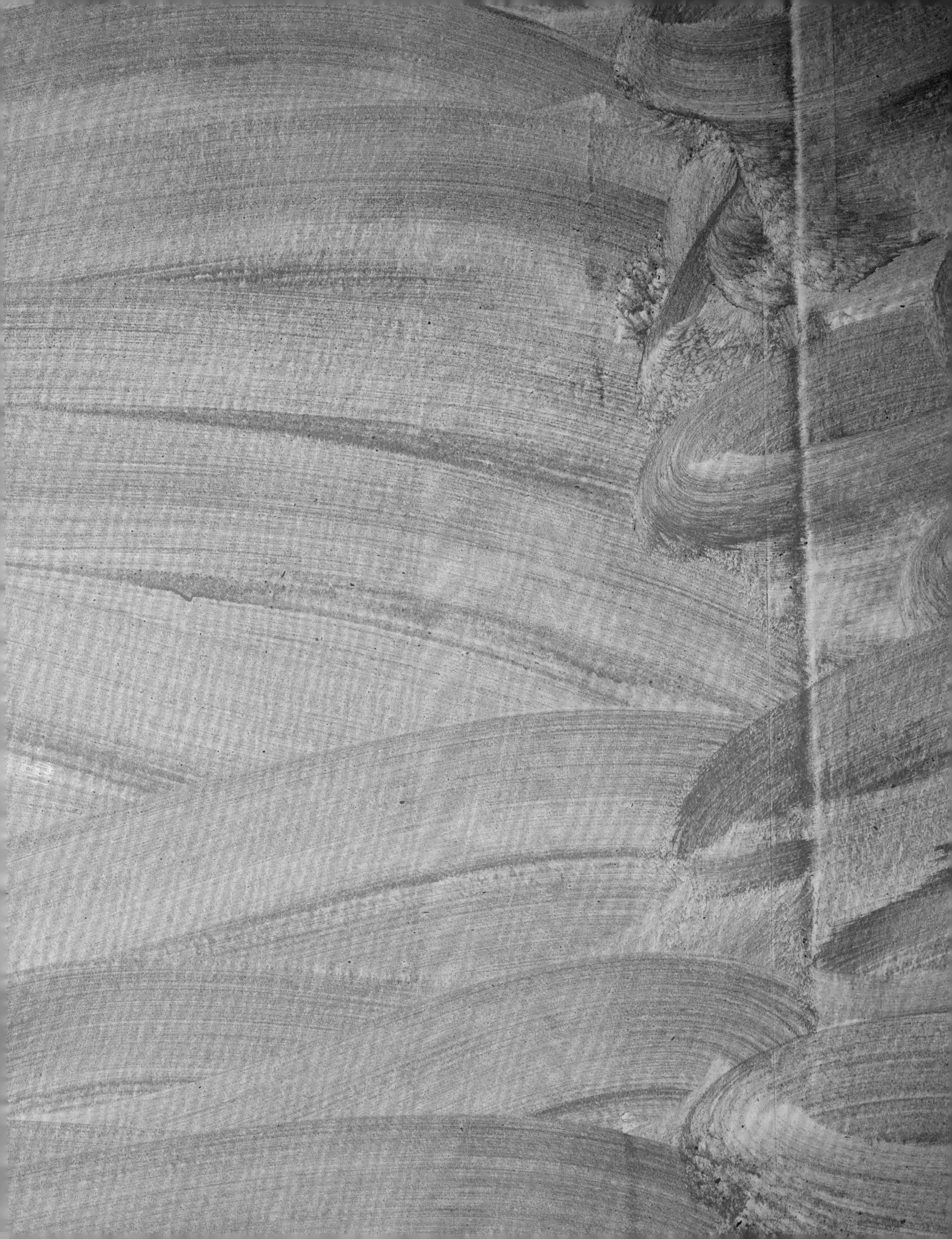

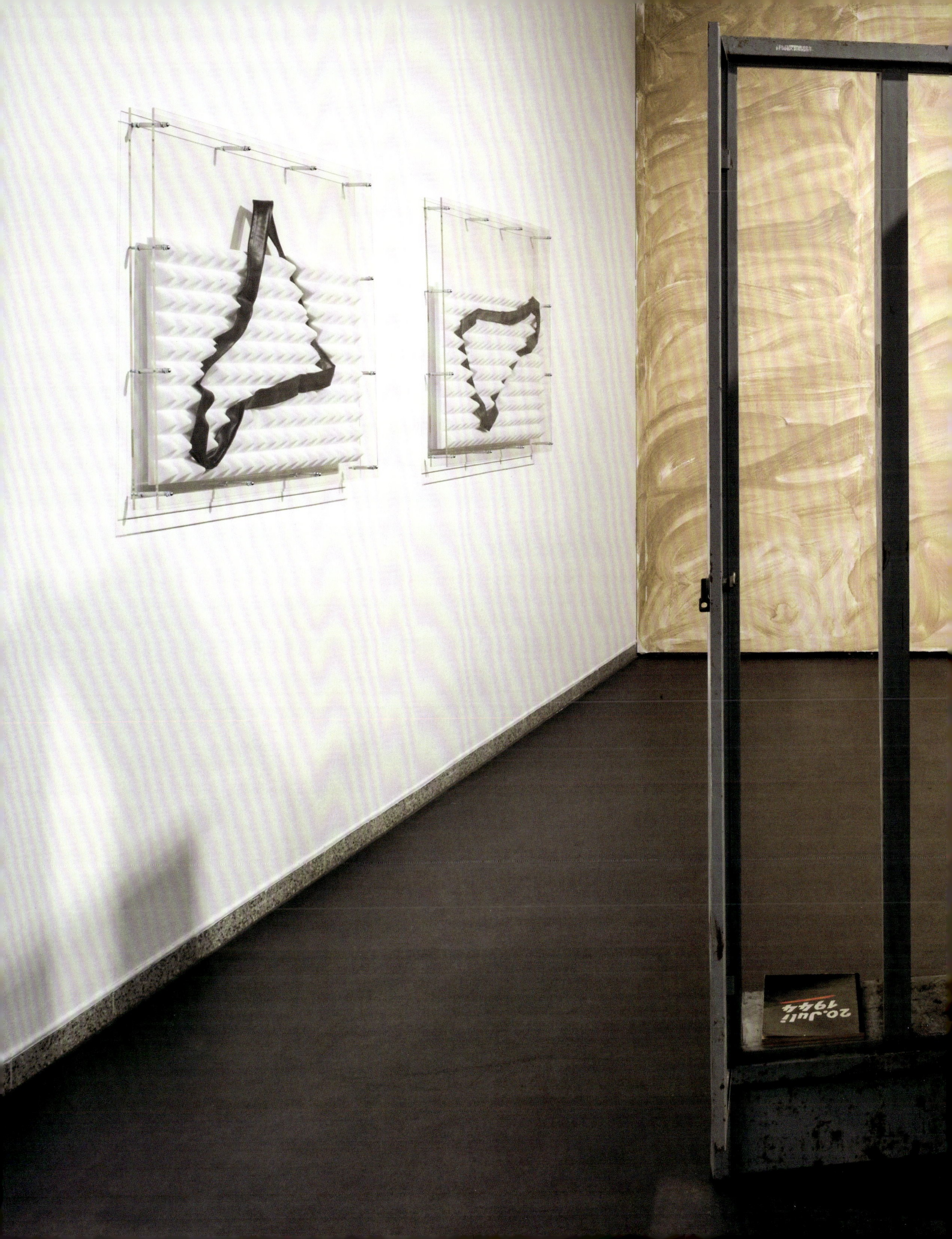
20.Juli
1944

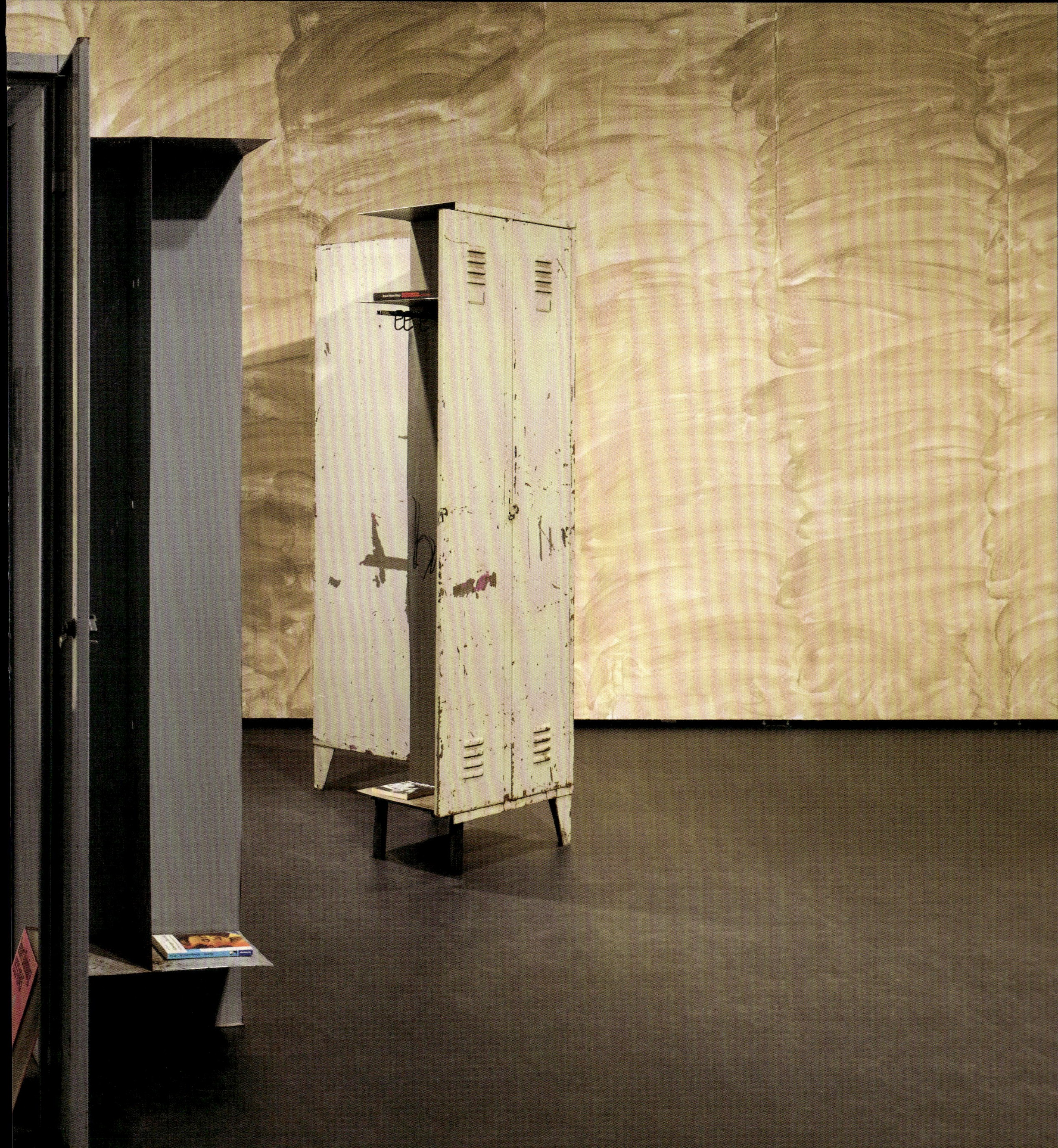

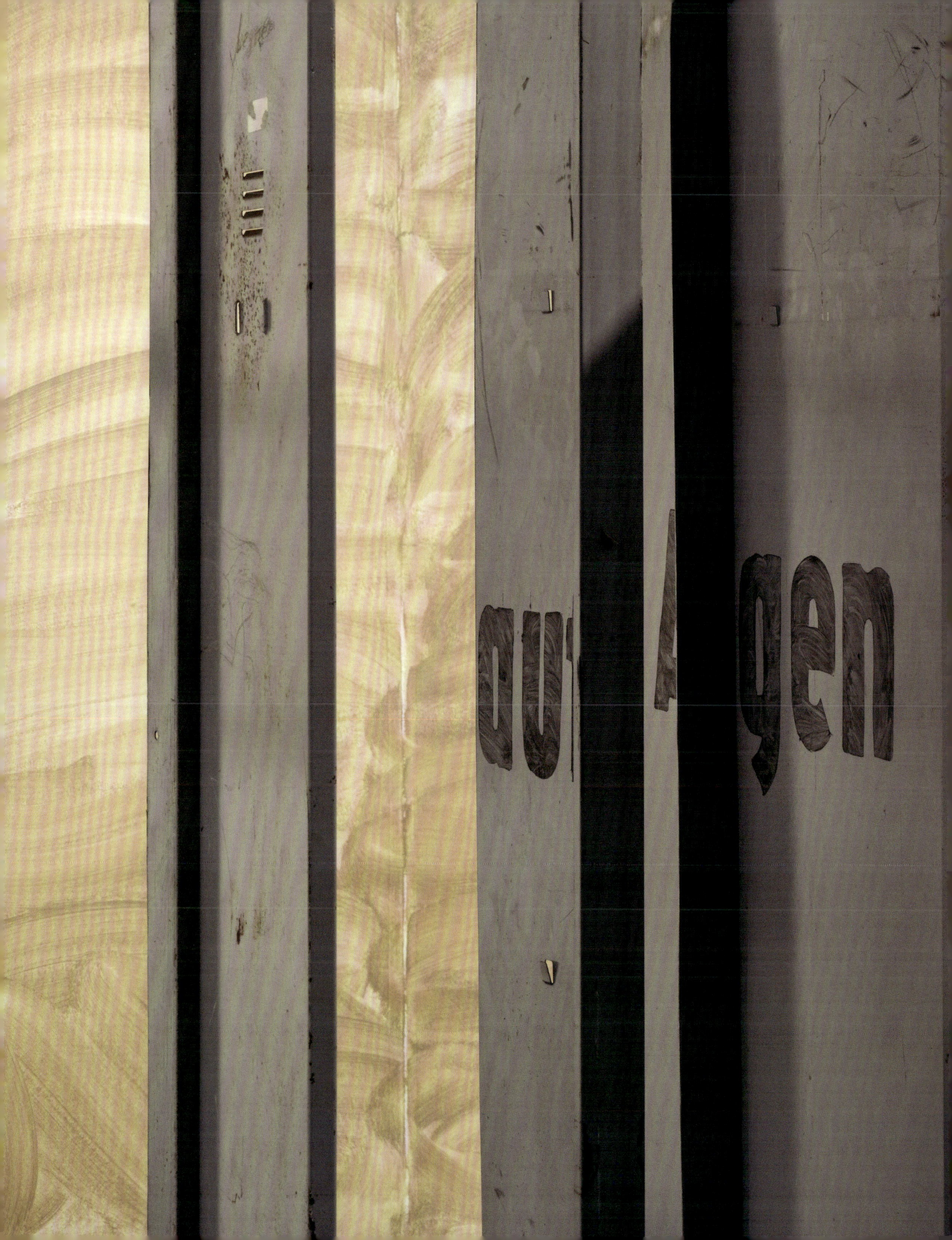
ou
gen

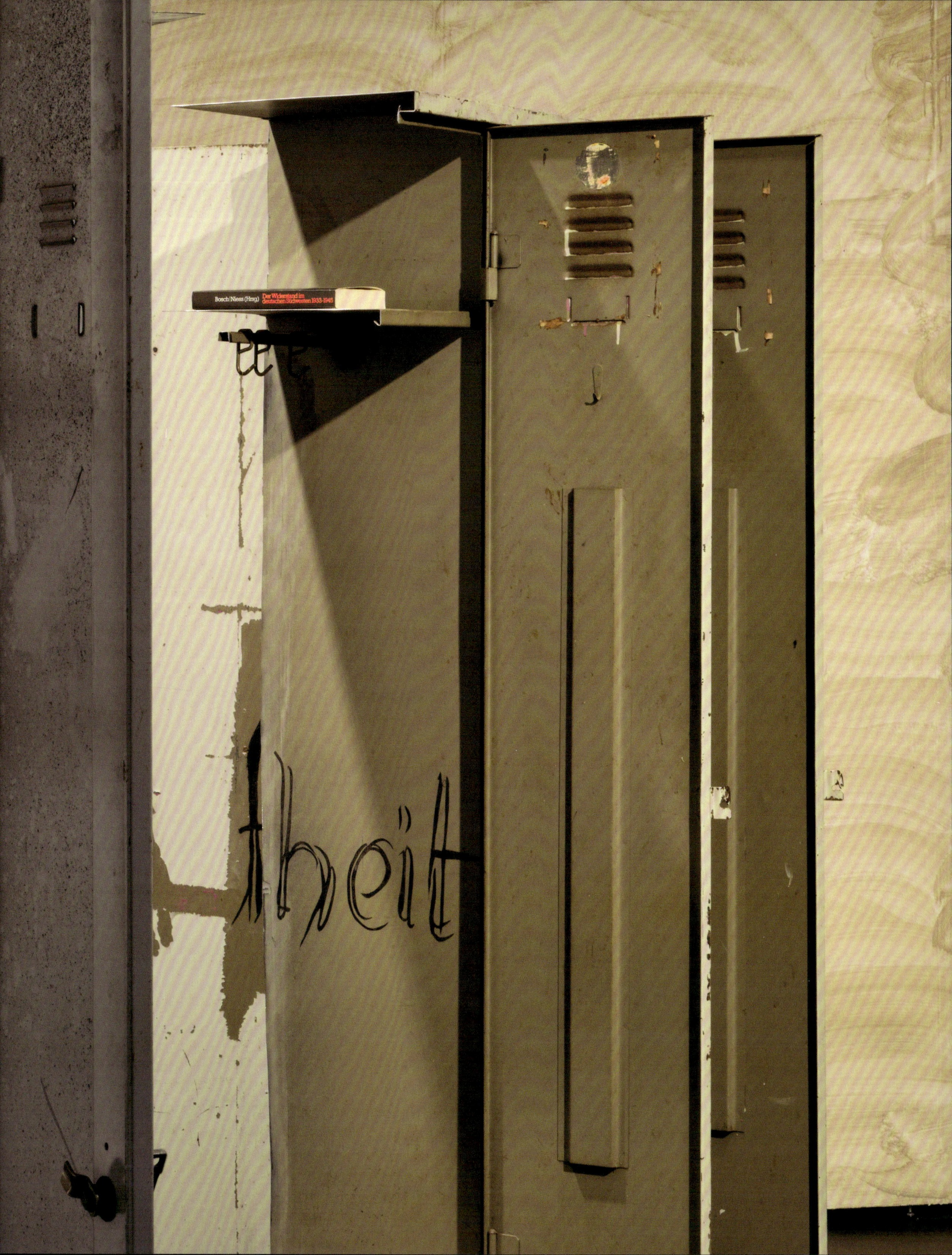
Bosch|Niess (Hrsg)
Der Widerstand im deutschen Südwesten 1933-1945
heit

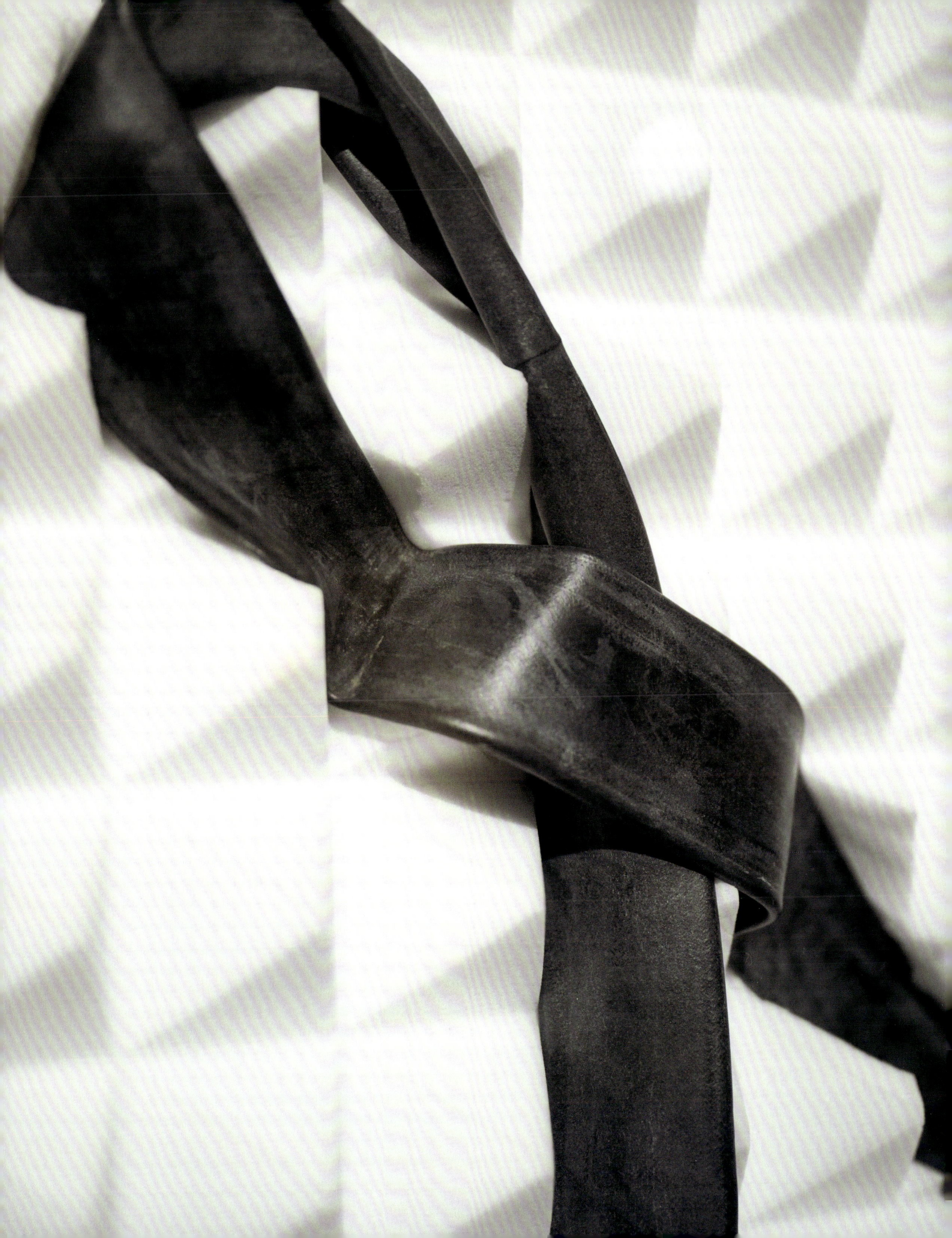

29

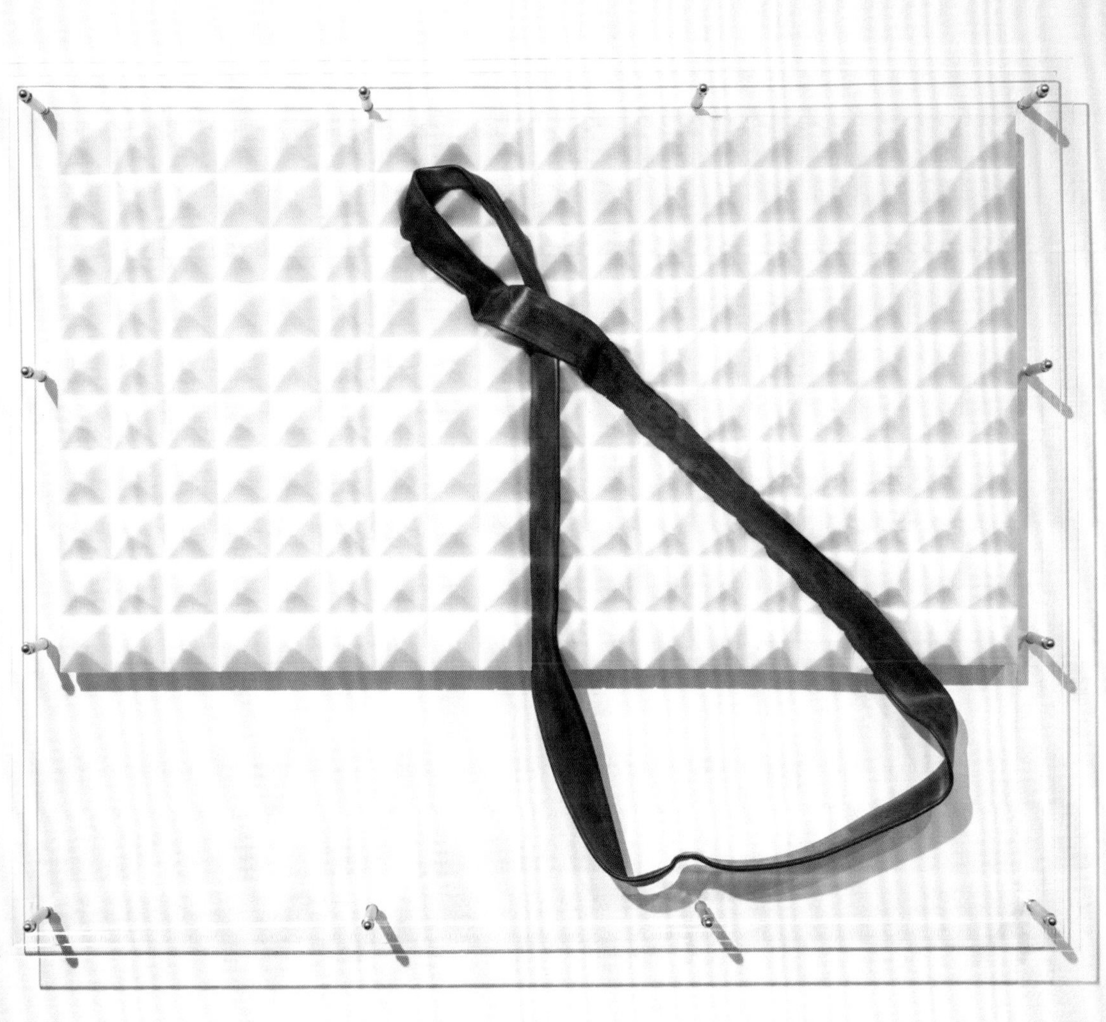

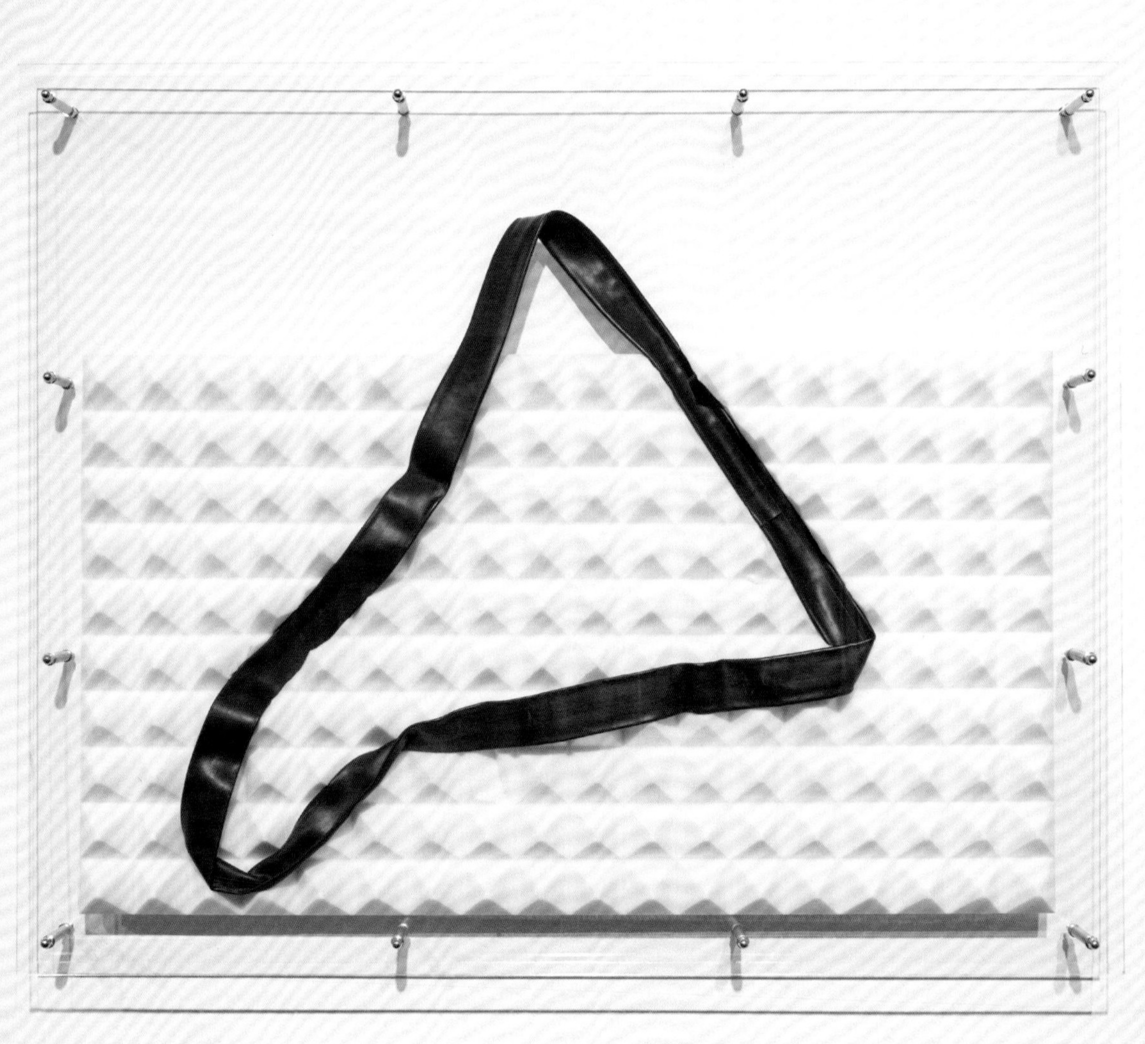

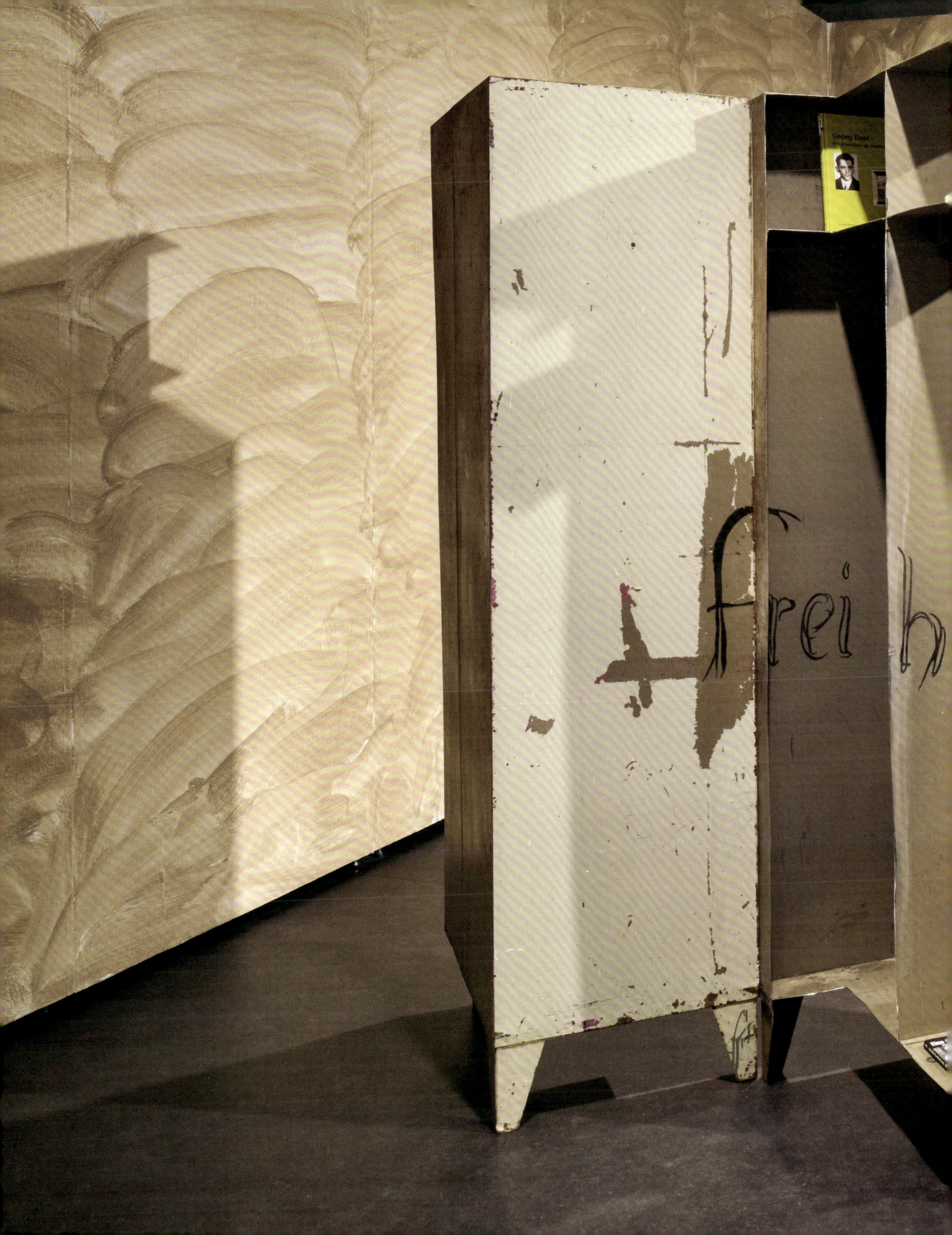
Georg Elser
frei

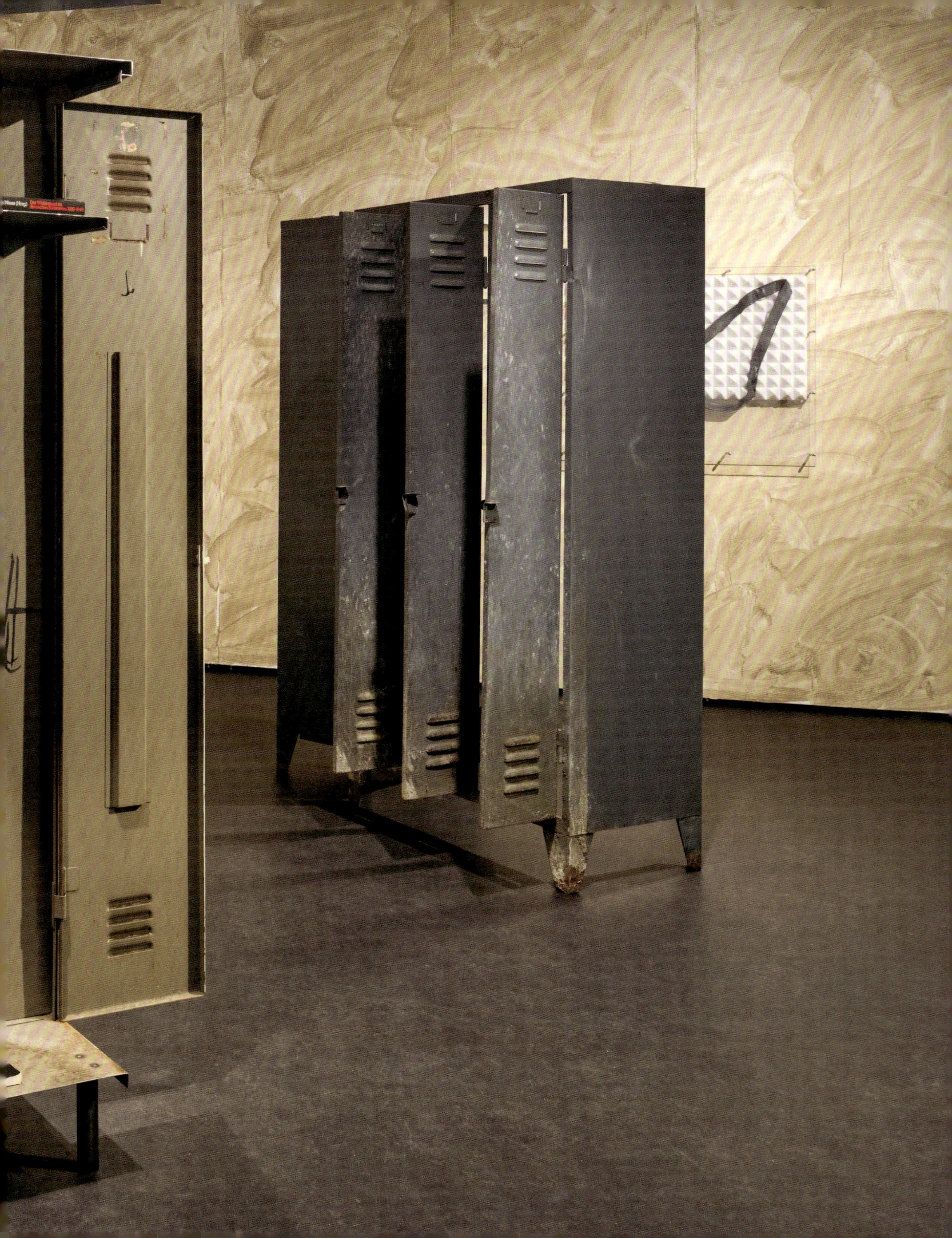

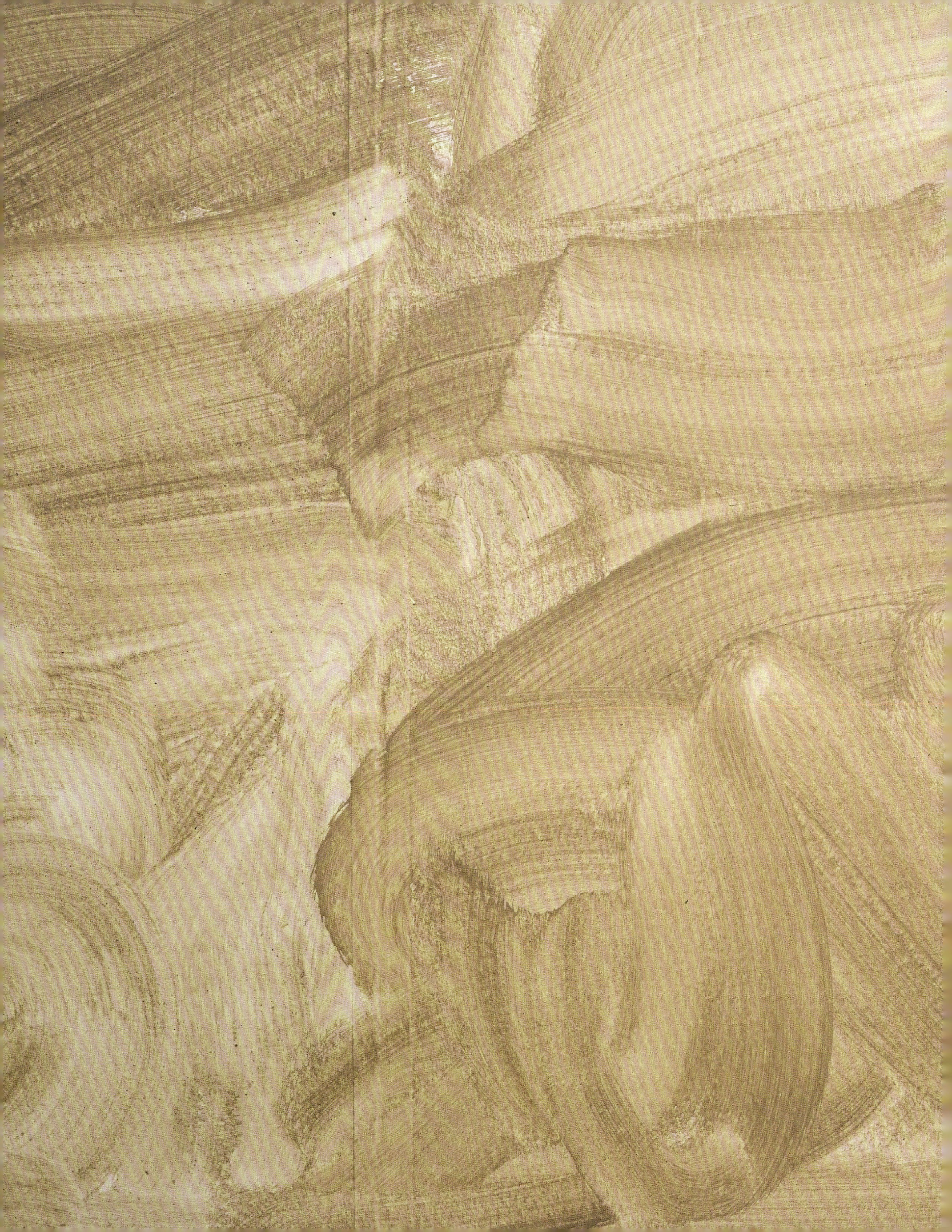

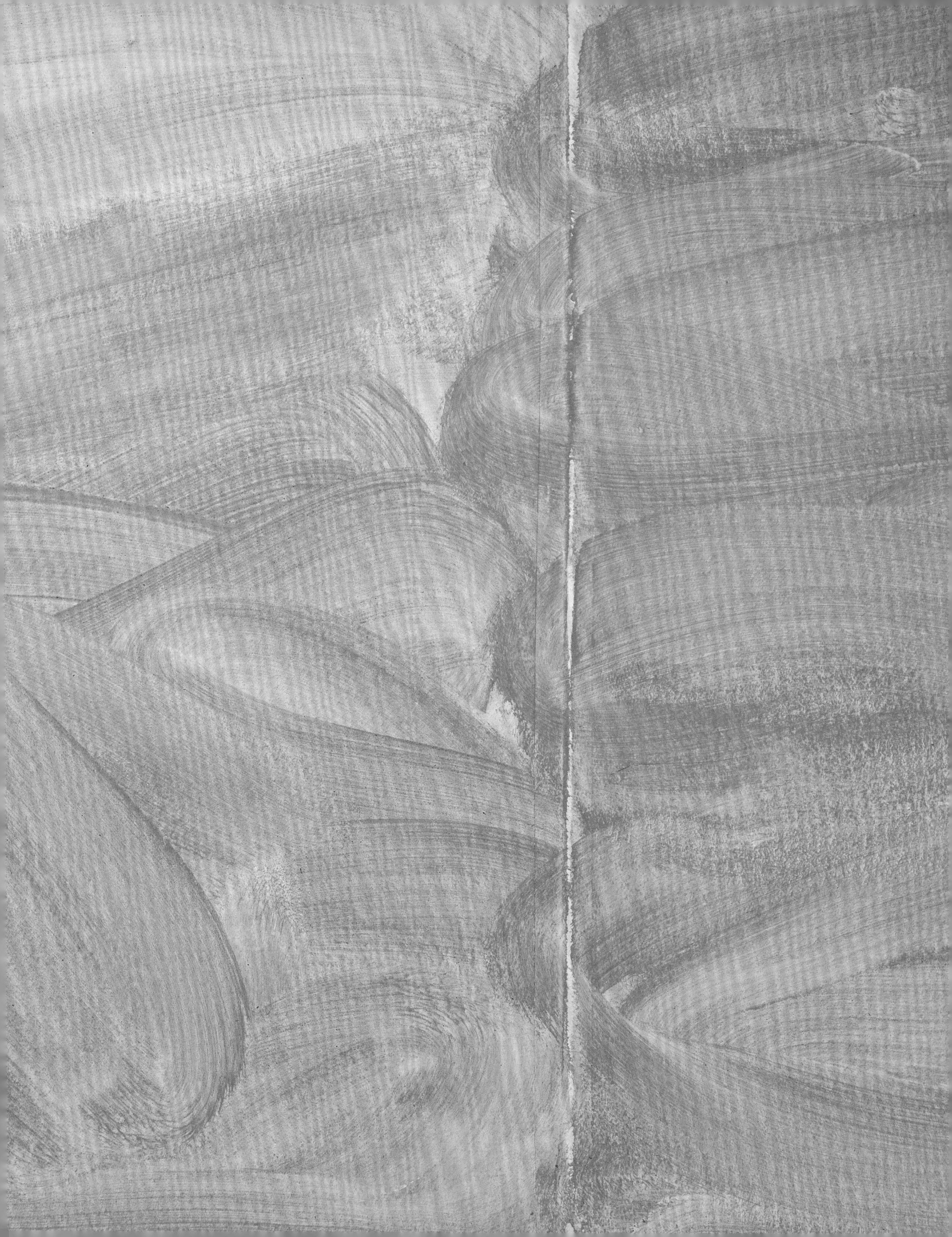

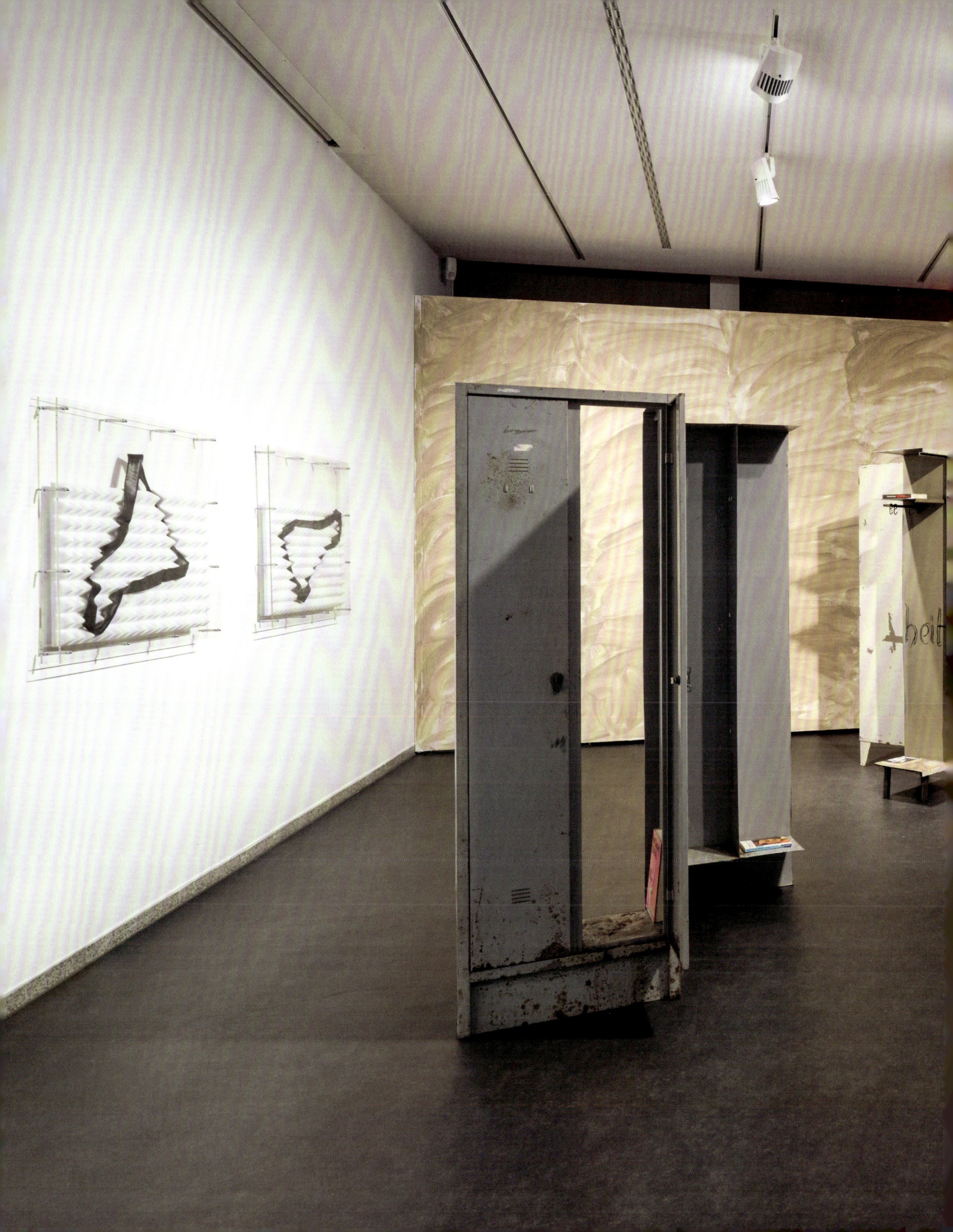

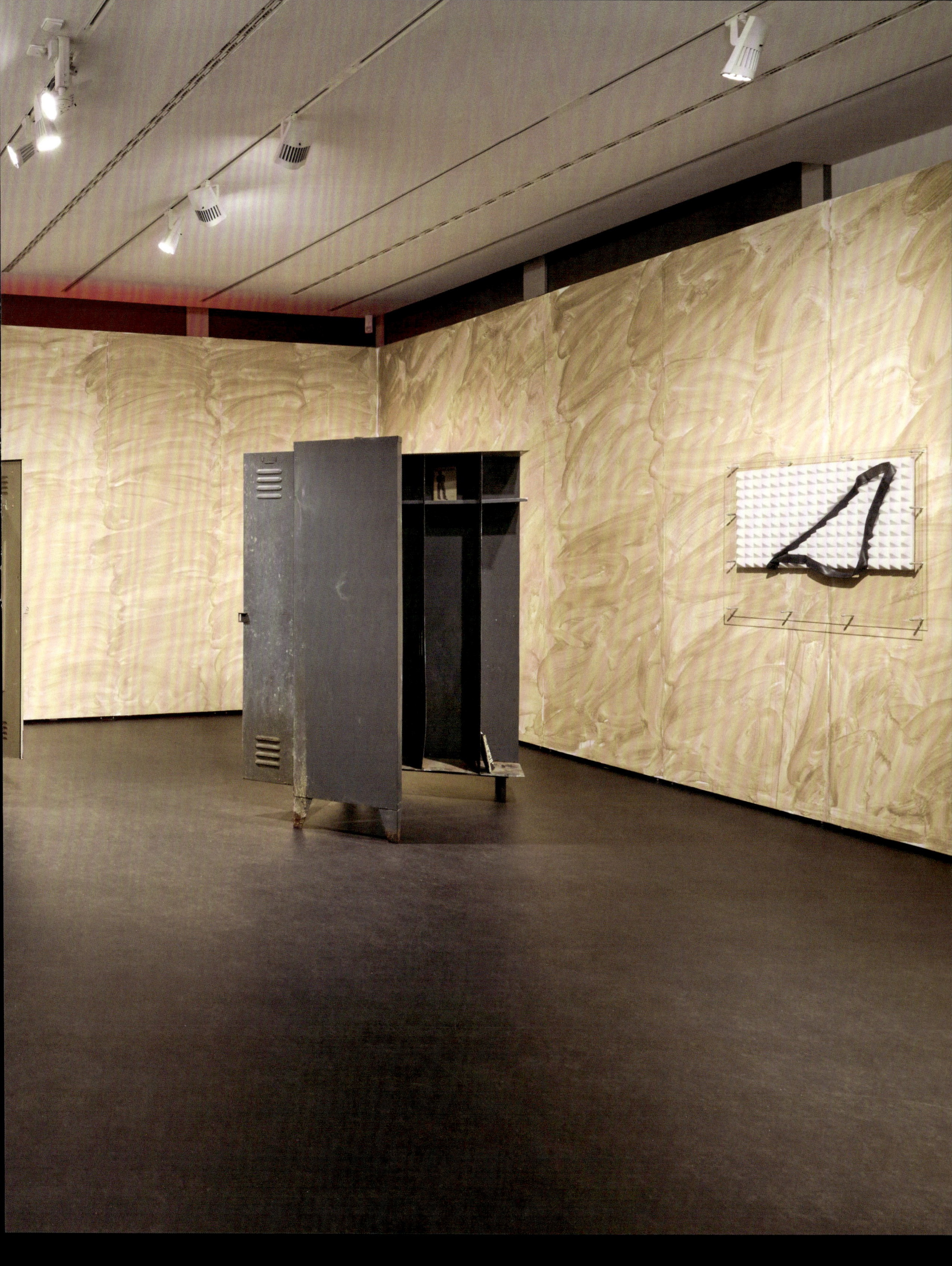

38

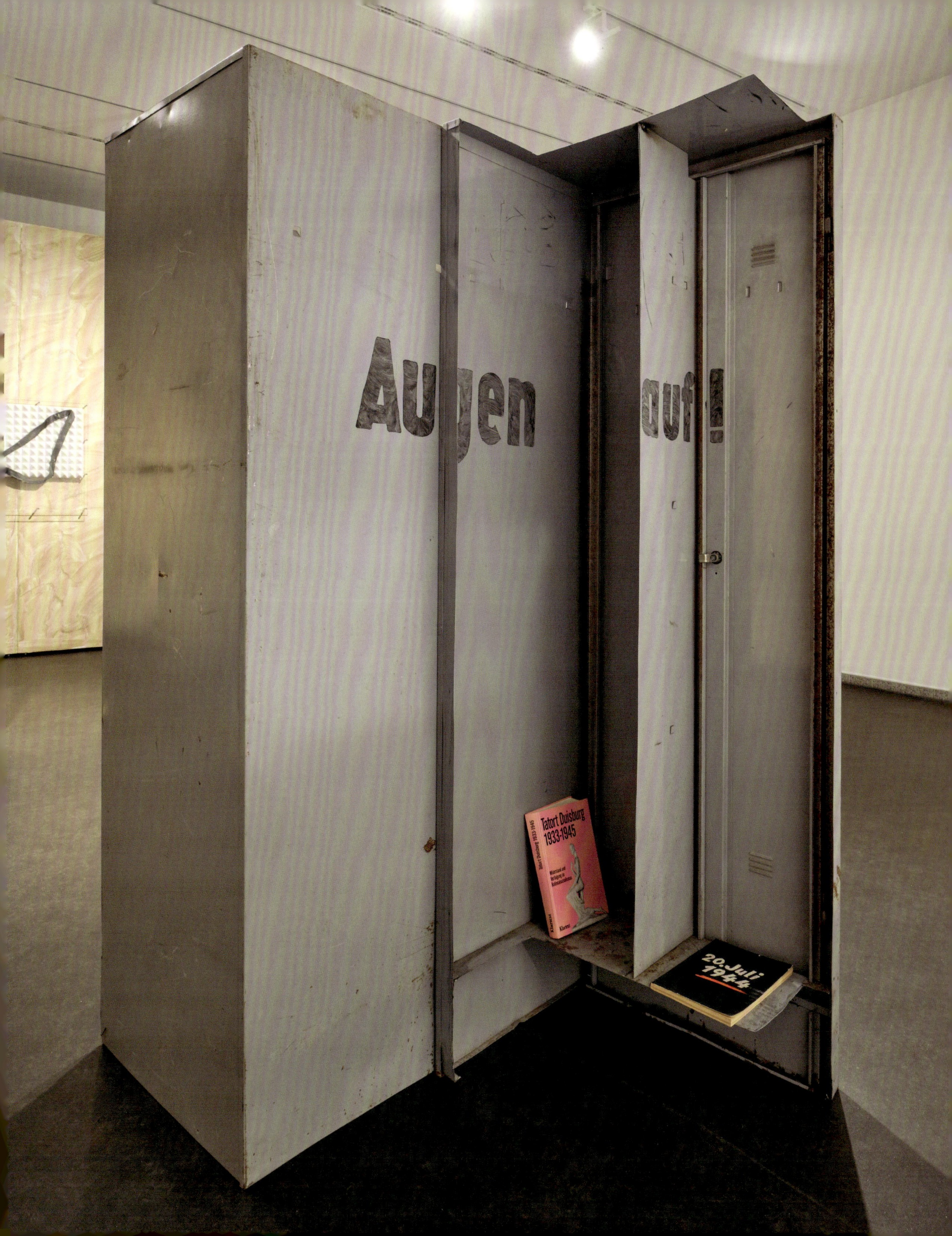

Augen auf!
Tatort Duisburg
1933-1945
20.Juli
1944

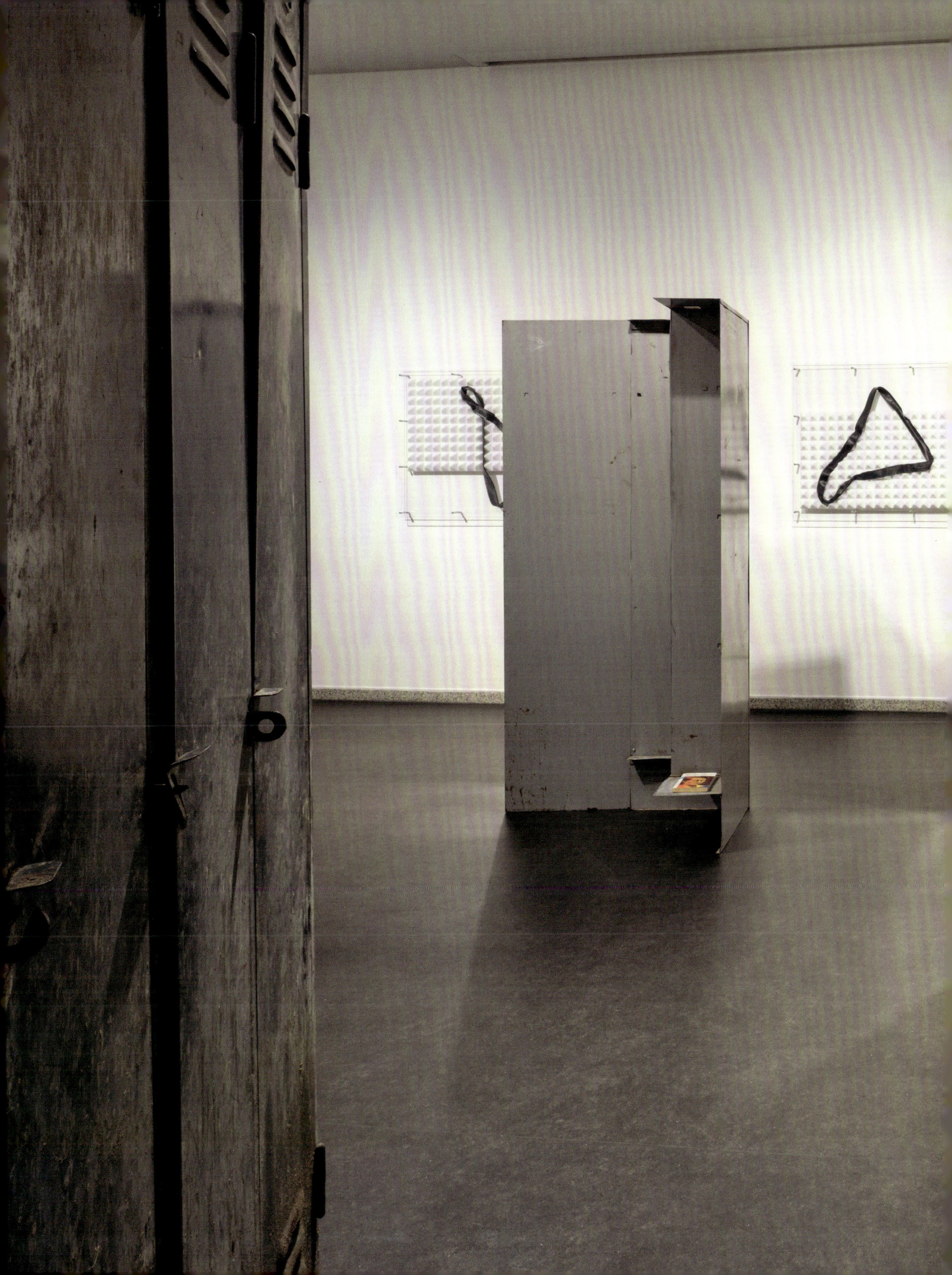

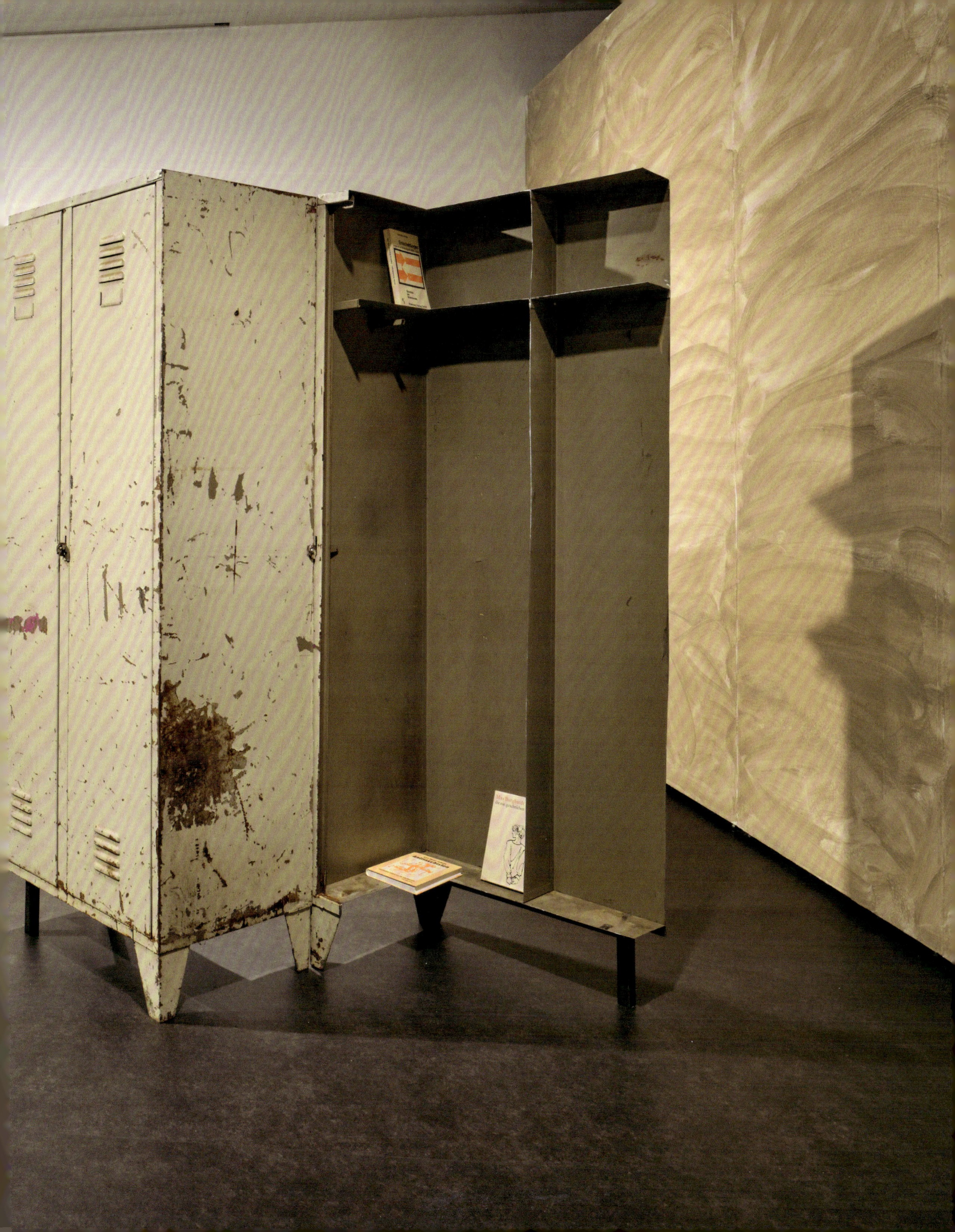

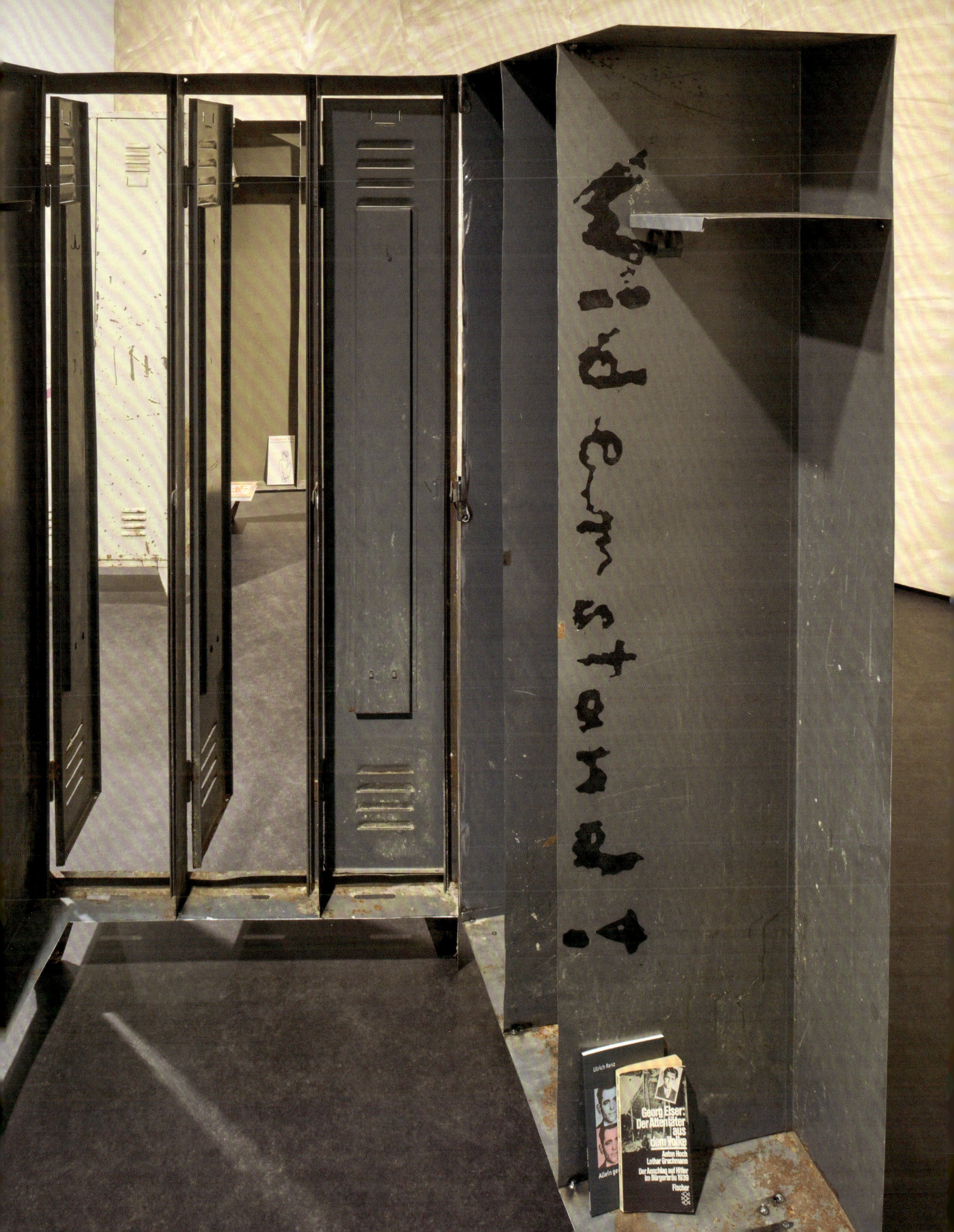
widerstand!
Ulrich Renz
Georg Elser: Der Attentäter aus dem Volke
Anton Hoch
Lothar Gruchmann
Der Anschlag auf Hitler im Bürgerbräu 1939
Fischer

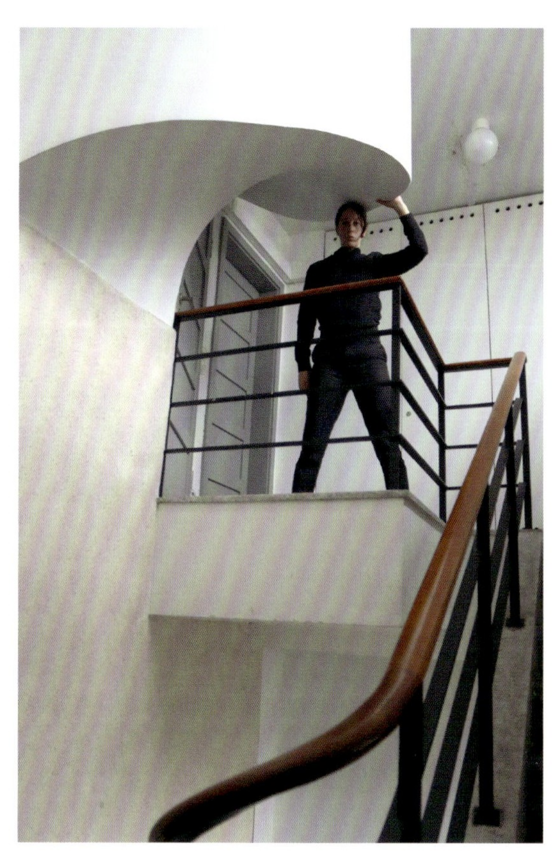

Werkliste

Paravent Körper
Drei dekonstruierte Spinde von Industriearbeitern; vergrößerte Faksimiles von Schriften von Widerstandskämpfern: Korrespondenzen, Broschüren und Tarnschriften, mit schwarzer Schuhfarbe auf die Metalloberfläche der Schließfächer aufgetragen; ausgewählte Bücher zur Dokumentation der lokalen und deutschlandweiten Widerstands-, Antifaschisten- und Arbeiterbewegung 1940–1945, die die Ausstellungsbesucher:innen herausnehmen und lesen können; 185 cm hoch, verschiedene Längen und Tiefen, Metall, 2023
Abb. S. 1, 14–21, 24–27, 32–33, 36–42, 46

Unheimliches Territorium
Wandmalerei, Schlamm aus dem KZ-Außenlager Dachau in Raderach, Friedrichshafen und vom Testgelände der Luftschiffbau Zeppelin GmbH Friedrichshafen für die „Wunderwaffe“, eine A4-Rakete; heute eine unmarkierte Ruine im Wald
Abb. S. 2, 22–23, 34–35, 45

Wache
Serie von Fotos (Selbstporträts), die die Künstlerin während ihres Aufenthalts im Zeppelin-Museumsturm aufgenommen hat, 2023
Abb. S. 4, 43

There Is Always Someone Looking Through The Window From This Tower
Neonschild an der Rückwand des Ausstellungsraums, von der Promenade aus gesehen;
150 × 36 × 4 cm, Plexiglas, Metall, 2023
Abb. S. 5, 9

Ortsrecherche von Luiza Margan
Zeigt Teile des ehemaligen Testgeländes der A4-Rakete der Firma Luftschiffbau Zeppelin GmbH Friedrichshafen; heute eine unmarkierte Ruine im Wald, 2023
Abb. S. 6

Schnitte durch die Stille
100 × 80 × 5 cm, Plexiglas, Akustikschaum, Butyl (Fahrradschläuche), Metall, 2023
Abb. S. 13, 28–31

List of Works

Paravent Body
Three reconstructed industrial workers' lockers, enlarged facsimiles of words taken from resistance fighters' correspondences, pamphlets, and covert letters, applied on the metal surface of the lockers with black shoe paint, selected books documenting the German Resistance-, Anti-Fascist and Workers' Movement 1940–1945 that exhibition visitors can take out and read; 185 cm high, various lengths and depths, metal, 2023
Figs. pp. 1, 14–21, 24–27, 32–33, 36–42, 46

Uncanny Territory
Wall painting, mud from the KZ-Subcamp Dachau in Raderach, Friedrichshafen, and the Luftschiffbau Zeppelin GmbH Friedrichshafen test site for the "Wunderwaffe," the A4 rocket; today an unmarked ruin in the forest
Figs. pp. 2, 22–23, 34–35, 45

Guard
A series of photographs (self-portraits) taken by the artist during the residency at the Zeppelin Museum Tower, 2023
Figs. pp. 4, 43

There Is Always Someone Looking Through The Window From This Tower
Neon sign mounted on back wall of exhibition space, visible from the promenade; 150 × 36 × 4 cm, Plexiglas, metal, 2023
Figs. pp. 5, 9

Site research photograph by Luiza Margan
Showing the former test site for the A4 rocket from the company Luftschiffbau Zeppelin GmbH Friedrichshafen; today an unmarked ruin in the forest, 2023
Fig. p. 6

Cut-through Silence
100 × 80 × 5 cm, Plexiglas, acoustic foam, butyl (inner bike tubes), metal, 2023
Figs. pp. 13, 28–31

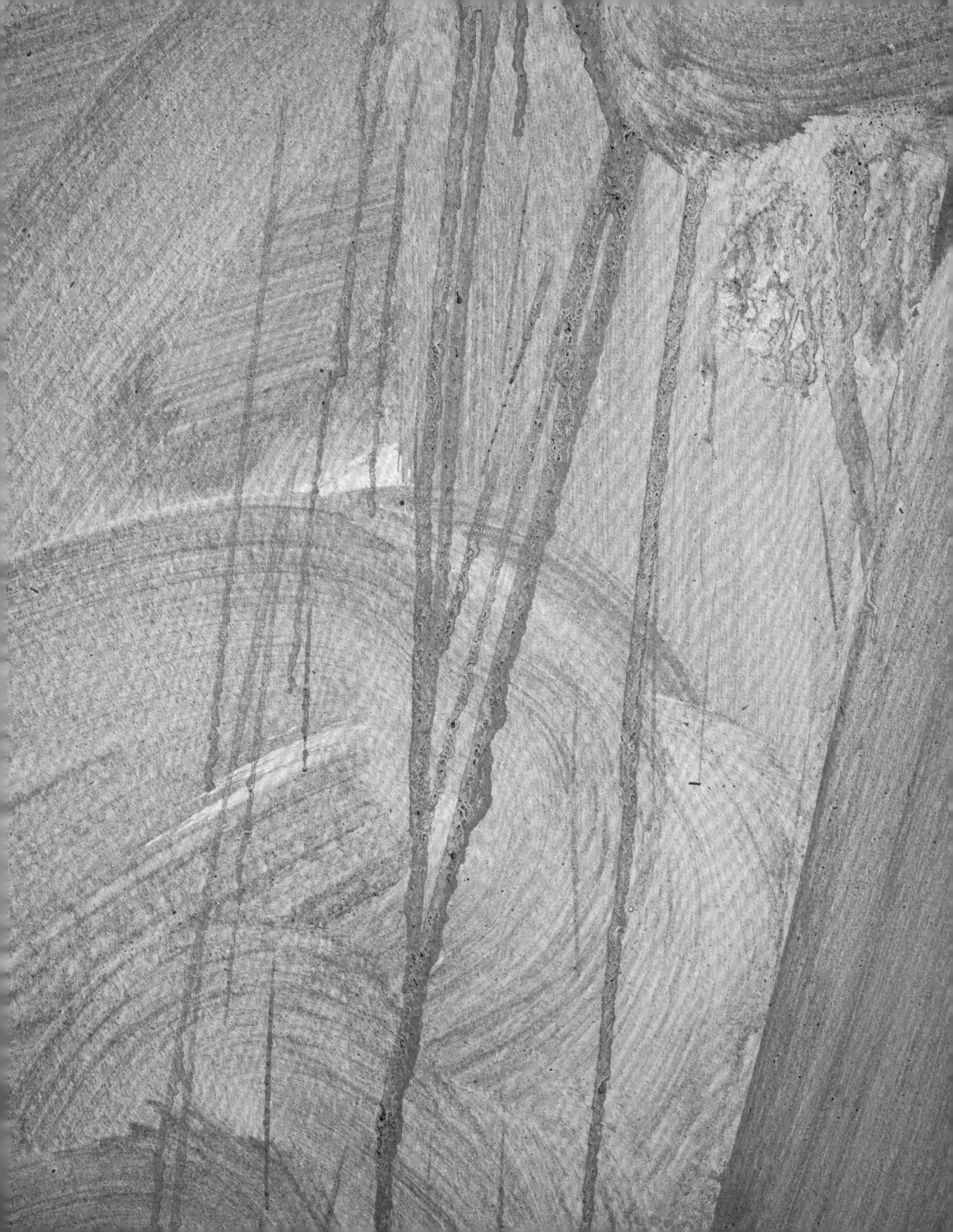

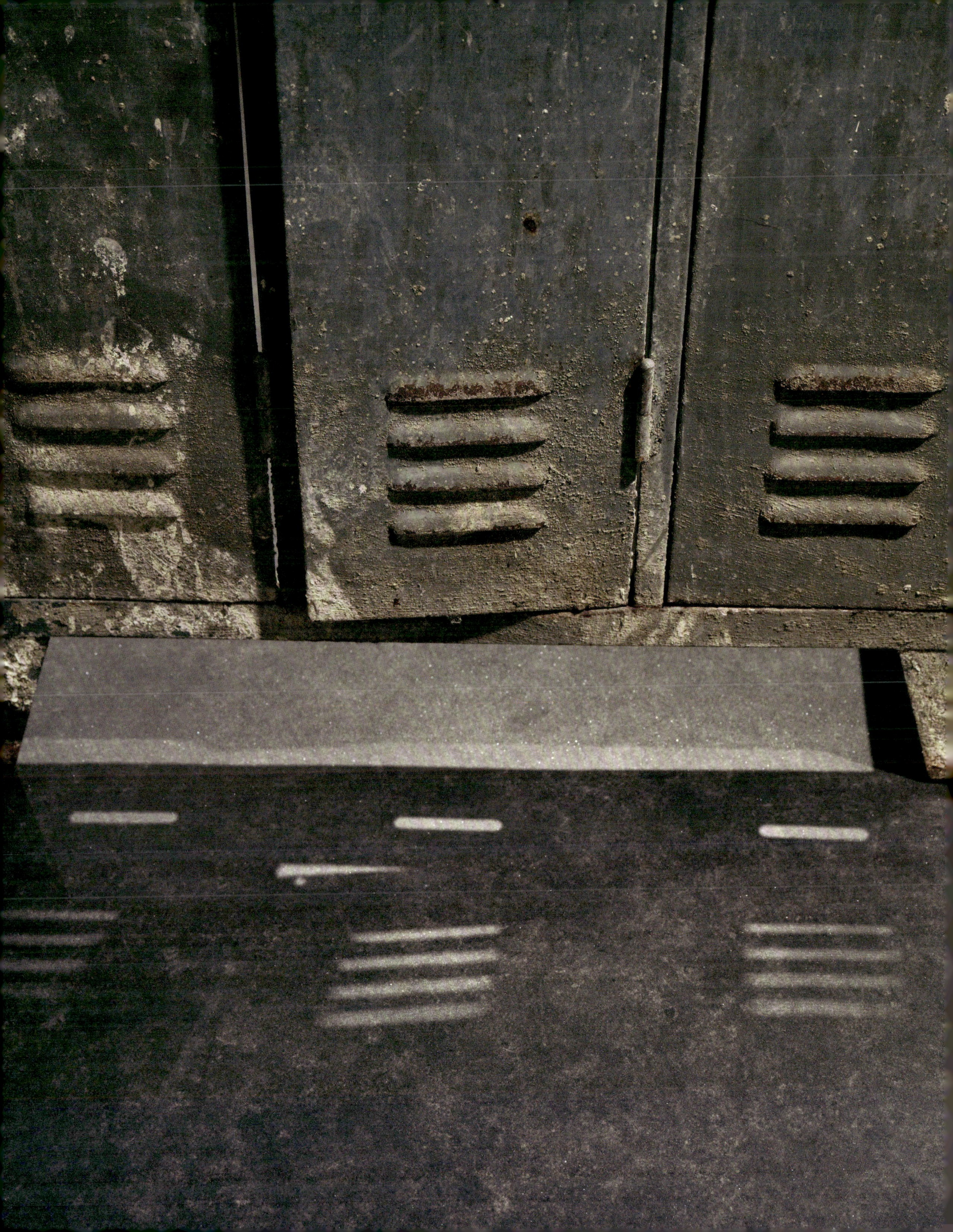

Biografie

Luiza Margan wurde in Rijeka, Kroatien, geboren und lebt derzeit in Wien. Sie studierte Malerei in Ljubljana, Slowenien, und Performative Kunst und Bildhauerei an der Akademie der bildenden Künste Wien, Österreich.

Mit ihren Skulpturen, Installationen, Filmen und Interventionen im öffentlichen Raum untersucht sie die Diskrepanz zwischen offizieller Geschichtsschreibung und unsichtbaren Geschichten, Machtverhältnissen und ideologischen Systemen, die in den öffentlichen Raum und das kollektive Gedächtnis eingeschrieben sind. Ihre Arbeit entsteht aus Feldforschung, historischem Material und dem performativen Einsatz des eigenen Körpers. Durch das Sammeln und Rekontextualisieren gefundener Materialien konstruiert sie neue Objekte, schafft neue Umgebungen und Sichtweisen.

Die Künstlerin hat in zahlreichen internationalen Museen und Galerien ausgestellt und hochgelobte künstlerische Veranstaltungen und Performances im öffentlichen Raum ins Leben gerufen. Ihre Werke sind in internationalen öffentlichen und privaten Kunstsammlungen vertreten, u. a. im Museum der Moderne in Salzburg, im Belvedere 21. Museum für zeitgenössische Kunst Wien, in der MUSA – Kunstsammlung der Stadt Wien, im Museum für zeitgenössische Kunst, Zagreb, und im Tabakmuseum, Ljubljana.

Neben zahlreichen Auszeichnungen erhielt Margan 2008 das Fellowship des International Studio & Curatorial Program (ISCP) in New York sowie 2019 das Stipendium für Visuelle Kunst und Medien der Akademie Schloss Solitude in Stuttgart. Im Jahr 2023 war Luiza Margan Artist-in-Residence der ZF Kunststiftung in Friedrichshafen.

Luiza Margan was born in Rijeka, Croatia, and is currently based in Vienna. She studied painting in Ljubljana, Slovenia, and Performative Arts and Sculpture at the Academy of Fine Arts Vienna.

Through her sculptures, installations, films, and interventions in public space, Margan examines the discord between official and invisible histories, power relations, and ideological systems inscribed in public space and collective memory. Her work emerges from field research, historical material, walking, and the performative use of her own body. By collecting and recontextualizing found materials, she constructs new objects, creating new environments and ways of seeing.

The artist has exhibited at numerous international museums and galleries, and has launched highly acclaimed artistic events and performances in public spaces. Her works are represented in international public and private art collections, including the Museum der Moderne Salzburg, the Belvedere 21. Museum for Contemporary Art in Vienna, the MUSA – Art Collection of the City of Vienna, the Museum of Contemporary Art in Zagreb, and the Tobacco Museum in Ljubljana.

Margan has received numerous awards, including a fellowship at the International Studio & Curatorial Program (ISCP) in New York in 2008, and a stipendium for visual artists at the Akademie Schloss Solitude in Stuttgart in 2019. In 2023, Luiza Margan was an Artist-in-Residence at the ZF Art Foundation in Friedrichshafen, Germany.

Biography

Impressum

48

Colophon

Dieser Katalog erscheint anlässlich der Ausstellung *Luiza Margan. Cache* der ZF Kunststiftung im Zeppelin Museum Friedrichshafen vom 24. November 2023 bis 28. Januar 2024.
This catalog is published on the occasion of the exhibition *Luiza Margan: Cache* held by the ZF Art Foundation at the Zeppelin Museum Friedrichshafen, from November 24, 2023 to January 28, 2024.

Herausgeber:innen Editors:
Matthias Lenz, Regina Michel,
ZF Kunststiftung, 88038 Friedrichshafen,
www.zf-kunststiftung.com
Redaktion Managing editor: Regina Michel
Redaktionsassistenz Assistant editor:
Talina Palmer
Text Text: Nora Sternfeld
Übersetzung Translation:
Katherine Vanovitch
Lektorat Copyediting:
Susann Harring (DE), Sarah Quigley (EN)
Gestaltung Design:
HFS Studio, www.hfs-studio.com
Herstellung Production:
Jens Bartneck, Kerber Verlag
Projektmanagement Project management:
Lydia Fuchs, Kerber Verlag

Installationsansichten
Installation views: Rafael Krötz
Foto Photo: Luiza Margan (S. pp. 4, 6, 43)

Kerber Verlag
Detmolder Straße 60
33604 Bielefeld, Germany
+49 521 950 08 10
+49 521 950 08 88 (F)
info@kerberverlag.com
kerberverlag.com

Kerber Publikationen werden weltweit vertrieben Kerber publications are distributed worldwide:

ACC Art Books
Sandy Lane
Old Martlesham
Woodbridge, IP12 4SD, UK
+44 1394 38 99 50
+44 1394 38 99 99 (F)
uksales@accartbooks.com
accartbooks.com

Artbook | D.A.P.
75 Broad Street, Suite 630
New York, NY 10004, USA
+1 (212) 627-1999
+1 (212) 627-9484 (F)
orders@dapinc.com
artbook.com

AVA Verlagsauslieferung AG
Centralweg 16
8910 Affoltern am Albis
Switzerland
+41 44 762 42 50
+41 44 762 42 10 (F)
avainfo@ava.ch

Zeitfracht Medien GmbH
Distribution
Germany
+49 711 7860 2254
bestellung@zeitfracht.de

Die Deutsche Nationalbibliothek verzeichnet diese Publikation in der Deutschen Nationalbibliografie; detaillierte bibliografische Daten sind im Internet über http://dnb.dnb.de abrufbar.
The Deutsche Nationalbibliothek lists this publication in the Deutsche Nationalbibliografie; detailed bibliographic data are available online at http://dnb.dnb.de.

www.kerberverlag.com

Printed in Germany
ISBN 978-3-7356-0968-7

Luiza Margan,
www.luizamargan.net

AF618078